Engineering For Passionate Beginners

Amelia E. Moreno

Introduction

This is a comprehensive introductory guide designed to provide young readers with a foundational understanding of various engineering disciplines. The book aims to inspire and educate teenagers who are interested in pursuing a career in engineering, offering valuable insights into the diverse fields of chemical, civil, electrical, and mechanical engineering.

The book begins with an engaging introduction to the field of engineering, providing an overview of its history and significance. It emphasizes the importance of engineering in driving innovation and solving real-world challenges, setting the stage for a comprehensive exploration of different engineering disciplines.

Each section of the book focuses on a specific engineering discipline, such as chemical, civil, electrical, and mechanical engineering. Within each section, the book provides in-depth information about the respective engineering specialties, covering key concepts, principles, and practical applications. It offers insights into the challenges that engineers face within each discipline, highlighting the critical role of problem-solving and innovation in addressing complex engineering problems.

Throughout the book, the author encourages young readers to explore the various branches of engineering, showcasing the exciting opportunities and potential career paths available within each discipline. By presenting inspiring examples of innovation and providing a deep dive into the fundamental principles of each field, the book aims to ignite the passion and curiosity of aspiring young engineers.

This book not only serves as an educational resource but also as a source of motivation for teenagers interested in pursuing a career in engineering. With its engaging and informative content, the book seeks to nurture the enthusiasm of young readers and prepare them for the challenges and opportunities that await them in the dynamic and ever-evolving field of engineering.

Contents

Chapter 1
INTRODUCTION TO ENGINEERING

THINK OF ALL THE WAYS WE USE OUR CELL PHONES. Beyond making actual phone calls, we text, email, and video chat. We record music and videos and post them on any number of apps. We look up walking or driving directions, order food, find nearby coffee shops and gas stations, play games, listen to music and podcasts, read the news, and interact with people all over the globe. Cell phones have become indispensable to modern society, yet many of us don't know about the innovations that led to the modern cell phone. In fact, the existence of your cell phone would not have been possible without several important breakthroughs in chemical, electrical, civil, materials, and mechanical engineering.

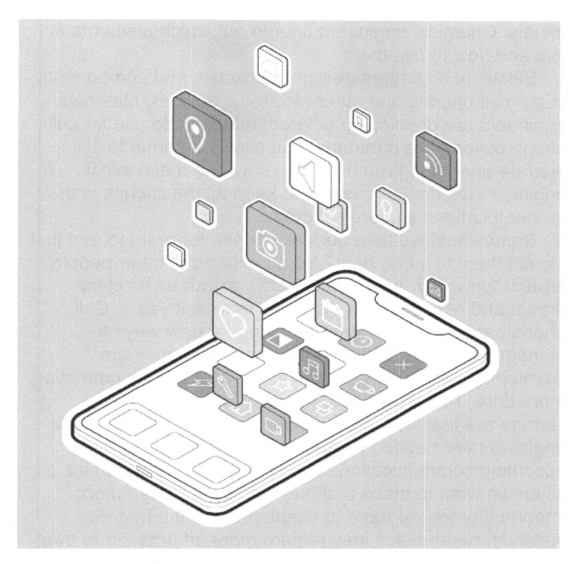

FIGURE 1: *Diagram of a smartphone and its apps*

About 84 percent of the non-radioactive elements in the periodic table are used in a smartphone, and there are more than 60 different metals. Some of these are rare earth metals. Chemical engineers figured out which elements to use and how to use them.

Electrical engineers design the circuits and components in our cell phones and other electronic devices. Materials engineers are developing different materials to use for cell phone covers, like a material that allows a phone to still operate after being run over by a car. And mechanical engineers design the casings to keep all the circuits in their proper locations and protect them.

Sometimes, we take our cell phones for granted and just expect them to work, right? So do millions of other people around the world. As a result, traffic growth on wireless broadband networks has exploded in recent years. Cell phone carriers are constantly looking for new ways to manage increased traffic. At the same time, they are developing new options to encourage you to consume even more data. To keep up with this ever-growing demand, carriers are installing more equipment. Civil and structural engineers are needed to support current networks and upcoming communications technology. This is important when we want to make a phone call, but it's even more important when we need to connect to the Internet. For instance, paramedics may require more information to treat individuals on-site and turn to their cell phones to find that information. Or a community may rely on cell phones to stay connected during a natural disaster, such as a hurricane or tornado. And consider this: What would your COVID-19 experience have been like without the Internet?

WHAT IS ENGINEERING?

Engineering is the use of math, science, and creativity to devise solutions to problems in order to benefit humankind and society. Engineers are inventors, innovators, scientists, builders, and explorers, taking ideas, concepts, and theories and using their scientific training and creative minds to turn those ideas into real-life applications. Engineers are responsible for giving us so much. Think about what you've used this week: The lights in your home. The car in your driveway and the roads it's traveled down. Your computer, TV, and other appliances. Food or drinks you've ingested. Medicine you've taken. Clothes you've worn or sports equipment you've used. There's a pretty good chance an engineer was behind every one of those things.

So, what does it mean to be an engineer? Every day, engineers work closely with many other talented innovators from different disciplines to solve problems or develop exciting new advances. This could mean designing driverless cars, developing computer technology for cell phone communications, or building bridges that can withstand hurricane-force winds. To be prepared to develop these solutions, engineers must learn math, science, and sometimes specialized knowledge such as medical principles to understand how to develop or improve physical and virtual systems.

Today, engineers in the medical field have helped develop artificial limbs and devices that improve our eyesight and hearing. Mobile communications and global connectivity designed by computer and software engineers allow us to interact with people who are thousands of miles away. This has made telemedicine available, in which people without immediate access to a doctor can still receive medical treatment. Transportation engineering has made it possible for us to travel from one part of the world to another within a day as opposed to weeks or even months.

HISTORY OF ENGINEERING

Engineering has had a significant impact on society for thousands of years, so its roots are ancient. Imhotep, an innovator who lived in ancient Egypt, is widely regarded as the first engineer. Imhotep designed the world's oldest standing stone monument, the step pyramid at Saqqara, Egypt. His principles have inspired workers around the world, from ancient Rome and Greece into the modern world.

As civilizations developed, people began reshaping their environment. Civilizations grew from farms to villages to some of the great cities in history. This growth was largely due to the roads and ships designed and built by engineers. Along with these great cities came new challenges and problems that needed to be solved. Those who practiced engineering principles to solve these problems may not have held the title of engineer but are considered forerunners of the engineering disciplines. Two particularly noteworthy examples of this are Filippo Brunelleschi and Galileo Galilei.

Filippo Brunelleschi (1377–1446) was an Italian architect who built one of the most beautiful and structurally demanding works of architecture of all time: Florence's famous dome on the Santa Maria del Fiore cathedral. Building a dome was difficult. Engineering concepts of stress, strain, tension, and compression were not yet well understood. Many believed the dome would collapse under its own weight before the mortar had dried. Also, no dome of its size existed at the time, so there was nothing to refer to.

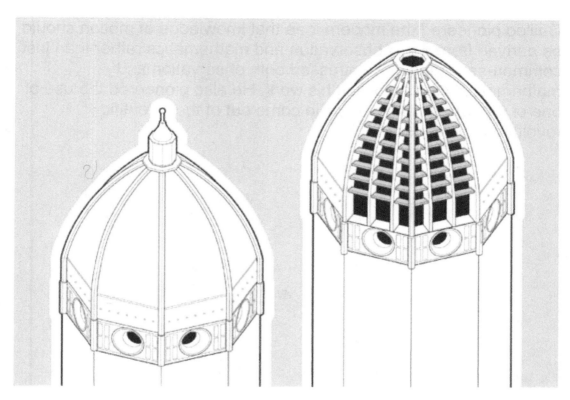

FIGURE 2: *Diagram of the dome on the Santa Maria del Fiore*

To help him succeed, Brunelleschi studied ancient architecture and applied mathematical principles developed by the ancient Egyptians and Greeks. Brunelleschi's solution was to design a hemispherical dome that could support its own weight as it was being built. He also invented a new device to hoist bricks to the top. He demonstrated good project management skills by encouraging his workers to bring their lunch up to the construction site to avoid wasting time and energy going up and down the many stairs. These seemingly minor adaptations are engineering problem-solving tools that have been carried throughout the profession to today.

Galileo Galilei (1564–1642) was a notable member of a period of rapid innovation that historians have called the scientific revolution.

Galileo pioneered the modern idea that knowledge of motion should be derived from direct observation and mathematics rather than just common-sense logic. He stressed both observation and mathematical calculations in his work. He also pioneered the use of one of the greatest inventions to come out of the scientific revolution: the telescope.

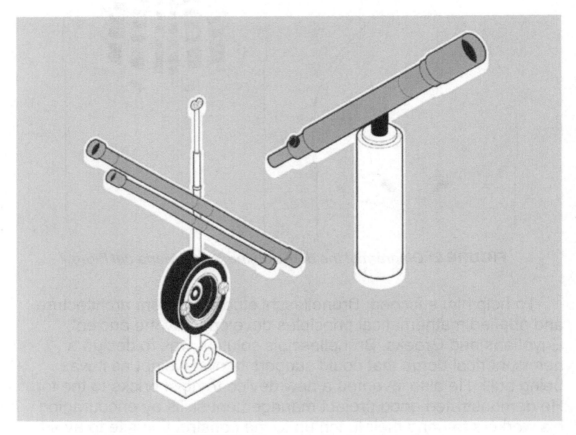

FIGURE 3: *Diagram of a telescope*

The earliest engineering schools in the United States were started in the early 1800s, the first being the US Military Academy at West Point in 1802. Other engineering schools followed, including

Norwich University in Vermont in 1819 and Rensselaer Polytechnic Institute in New York in 1824. As the need to apply math and science to solve problems grew, so did the need for formal engineering education for a larger population. In 1865, with only 15 students, the Massachusetts Institute of Technology opened its doors for the first time. Many other great engineering schools would soon follow, offering many opportunities to study engineering throughout the country.

Also during the nineteenth century, new processes and methods —most notably in the petroleum field—reshaped transportation, construction, and manufacturing processes around the world. As a result, these technologies formed the beginning of many different industries. Innovations such as the continuous stage sewing machine, the cable car, and the telephone were developed. Their inventors began to identify with engineering processes, and specific disciplines began to emerge, forming the many engineering disciplines we have today.

The initial engineering disciplines were civil, mechanical, and electrical engineering. Individuals in these three broad disciplines began solving problems and impacting the world. Their contributions formed the basis of the industrial revolution of the twentieth century and modernized much of the world, especially the United States. One of the greatest engineering achievements was applying electrical principles so that homes could have electricity. This made homes more comfortable, more efficient, and safer. Electricity also allowed people to work longer, study more, and engage in social activities that previously would not have been possible. Also during this time, communication advances by way of the telephone, radio, and television gave us new ways to see ourselves in the world and connect in ways never before possible.

FAMOUS ENGINEERS IN HISTORY

Archimedes (b. 287 BCE): Archimedes is best known for inventing Archimedes's screw, a device to move water without heavy lifting. This innovation helped farmers irrigate their crops. Archimedes was also known for identifying one of the most fundamental concepts in physics, the center of gravity.

Leonardo da Vinci (b. 1452): Among da Vinci's many talents was engineering. He was responsible for numerous real and theoretical inventions. His engineering accomplishments include designing tanks, catapults, submarines, machine guns, and other weapons for the military. In 1495, he detailed plans for what is considered the first iteration of a robot!

Elijah McCoy (b. 1844): Elijah McCoy was born in Canada, but his family moved to the United States when he was a teen. He trained in Scotland as a mechanical engineer. As a Canadian Black man, he was unable to find a position as an engineer in the United States, so McCoy accepted a job with a railroad. There, he improved the railroad's operations by inventing a lubrication device to keep the trains' moving parts working properly.

Alexander Graham Bell (b. 1847): Best known as the inventor of the telephone in 1876, Alexander Graham Bell also owned Bell Telephone Company (which later became AT&T), was a co-founder of *Science* magazine, and served as president of the National Geographic Society.

Nikola Tesla (b. 1856): If you plugged something into a wall socket today, thank Austrian engineer Nikola Tesla. Tesla is best known for designing the electrical system used almost everywhere, the AC, or alternating current, system.

Edith Clarke (b. 1883): Edith Clarke was the first woman to be professionally employed as an electrical engineer in the United States. She worked as a "human computer" for AT&T and as an engineer for General Electric. She developed and patented a "graphical calculator" to help solve problems related to transmission lines.

Hedy Lamarr (b. 1913): Famous as a Hollywood film star in the 1930s, Hedy Lamarr was not only one of the most acclaimed actors of her time, she was also the coinventor of a communications technology that was an important stepping stone to the development of today's Bluetooth and Wi-Fi technologies.

Hattie Scott Peterson (b. 1913): Believed to be the first Black woman to earn a bachelor's degree in civil engineering, Hattie Scott Peterson later became the first woman to join the US Army Corps of Engineers, where she advocated for women in engineering careers.

Mary Jackson (b. 1921): Mary Jackson was the first Black female engineer at NASA. Her work focused on the airflow around aircraft. The story of her groundbreaking contributions to NASA, along with those of Katherine Johnson and Dorothy Vaughn, was dramatized in the 2016 film *Hidden Figures*.

Willie Hobbs Moore (b. 1934): The first Black woman to receive a PhD in physics, Willie Hobbs Moore worked as a research scientist at the University of Michigan. Later she moved to the Ford Motor Company, where she worked as an assembly engineer. Ford was incorporating different Japanese engineering methods, and Moore expanded their use.

William "Bill Nye the Science Guy" Nye (b. 1955): William Nye was a mechanical engineer at Boeing. While he was there, he invented the hydraulic pressure resonance suppressor tube used in the Boeing 747 airplanes. This device minimizes the effect of vibrations that get introduced into an airplane's system. He is perhaps best known for his TV personality, Bill Nye the Science Guy. He used that platform to educate younger generations of future engineers.

Alan Emtage (b. 1964): The use of search engines is so ever-present in our lives, it's hard to picture a world without them. Alan Emtage, a computer engineer from Barbados, developed what is widely considered the world's first search engine, called Archie, in 1989.

WHY BE AN ENGINEER?

If you ever thought you would like to have a positive impact on the world, a career in engineering could be a great place for you to start. If you become an engineer, you can solve important problems that improve your society and community. From designing innovative tablets and smartphones to changing the way we collect and store energy, engineers improve and advance how we live.

As an engineer, you could be working with other interesting people who are identifying and preventing pollution, changing the conditions that contribute to global warming, developing new medicines, advancing new communications technologies, or developing devices that help people walk who previously were wheelchair users. Engineers use their creativity and training to solve problems and find solutions that will improve our lives. So, as an engineer you have the power to make a difference.

Engineering is a team sport. Solving problems involves collaboration with people from all sorts of different backgrounds, from those in different engineering disciplines to doctors, architects, and artists. As an engineer, you'll also have the opportunity to work alongside other smart, talented, socially conscious people. Many engineering positions also offer opportunities to travel all over the world.

PREPARING FOR A CAREER IN ENGINEERING

Many entry-level engineering jobs only require a bachelor's degree, which usually takes four or five years to obtain. You can then go on to earn a master's or doctorate degree, which will increase your career opportunities as well as your earning potential.

To begin preparing for a career in engineering, it's best to start early, in middle school or high school. Identifying the engineering discipline that interests you means preparing yourself today and working toward building that engineering mindset so you're best prepared for your future. Some of the best math courses to consider in middle school or high school are algebra, geometry, trigonometry, and calculus. Science courses to consider are biology, chemistry, computer science, and physics.

However, academic and technical skills are not enough. As an engineer, you'll need great verbal and written communication skills as well as social skills in order to get your ideas across. Having an edge in graphic design can also be helpful.

One of the best ways to prepare for entering college to study engineering is to find pre-college programs. Pre-college programs come in many forms. They can include after-school programs, weekend programs, or summer programs. In addition to learning about different engineering disciplines, the benefits of programs like these include finding mentors, earning college credit, and finding scholarship opportunities.

If you live far from the college programs that you may be considering, that's okay. There are many organizations that offer online and virtual programs to introduce students to engineering. Consider joining clubs and organizations at your school or in your community that are associated with engineering or other STEM-related disciplines.

For now, let's dive in.

Chapter 2
CHEMICAL ENGINEERING

INSPIRING INNOVATION

In the United States, approximately 10 percent of infants are born prematurely each year. According to the Centers for Disease Control and Prevention, this rate is significantly higher than the rates of other developed countries, but some developing countries have even higher premature birth rates. Women in Malawi, a country in southeast Africa, experience the highest rate of premature births, at 18 percent. This is concerning because premature birth is the leading cause of infant mortality. It can also lead to ongoing health concerns and disabilities in surviving infants.

A team of bioengineering researchers specializing in medical applications at Stanford University has made advances here. They found a way to measure substances in a pregnant woman's blood that give a more reliable estimate of her due date. This chemically engineered process provides doctors with a safe technique to predict whether the baby will arrive prematurely.

When a woman is pregnant, some of the baby's DNA gets mixed into the mother's blood and DNA. Doctors can take a sample of the mother's blood and learn information about mother and baby. The test checks for certain DNA markers that have been shown to be associated with premature delivery.

In some cases, knowing there is a high risk of a baby arriving too soon can help save the child. Some premature babies just don't survive—they can be too small and underdeveloped. Other babies may be at risk of certain issues if they arrive too early. If these issues are known in advance, doctors may be able to help treat the baby before the premature delivery, increasing the child's chances of survival and avoiding lifelong medical conditions.

This new blood test has been expanded to identify other predictors. Now, doctors can do a blood test to check for the possibility of a baby having Down syndrome. A person with Down syndrome has an extra chromosome. This extra chromosome results in physical changes as well as problems with internal organs, such as the kidneys and heart. The test traditionally used for detecting Down syndrome is called amniocentesis. Amniocentesis involves a medical professional sticking a needle into a pregnant woman's uterus and extracting a fluid sample to be used to test for the syndrome. This is an uncomfortable and invasive procedure, and there is a risk for miscarrying as a result of having this test done. Now, thanks to the bioengineers at Stanford, the simple blood test is replacing amniocentesis.

Today, Stanford researchers also hope to be able to develop a blood test to see if a transplanted organ, such as a heart, is going to be rejected. The body does that sometimes because it doesn't recognize the new organ. The body thinks it's an invader of some kind and tries to get rid of it. The researchers are working on other blood tests that may help detect predictors of cancer or Alzheimer's disease.

How amazing will it be to use engineering to help prepare for the delivery of premature babies or help prevent a serious disease?

What advice would you give to someone who's thinking about becoming an engineer?

"I would recommend finding the industry/products that you relate to and are passionate about. Sometimes the day-to-day work can seem

unexciting, but if you can be proud of the finished product, it is all worth it."

—HUNTER HENDRICK, *materials developer*

DEEP DIVE

Chemicals are a huge part of our everyday lives, from the clothes we wear, the food we eat, and the water we drink to the vehicles we drive and, as you have already seen, to the cell phones we use to communicate. For more than a century, chemical engineers have been pioneering advances in medicine, public health and safety, and technology that improve our lives and society.

Chemical engineering combines the studies of chemistry, physics, microbiology, biochemistry, math, and economics. Broadly speaking, chemical engineers identify substances and materials that can be useful. Then they figure out how to make products from those materials. This often begins in a laboratory and then moves into the process of full-scale production. The result? Products related to everything from food to fashion end up on our shelves. Chemical engineers may also oversee the processes for developing products and can be involved in the construction and operation of chemical plants.

If this sounds like something you'd like to do, you're in luck. Chemical engineers are always in high demand because of the diverse and extensive industries that depend on the processing of chemicals and materials. In addition to traditional careers with chemical companies and the oil industry, chemical engineers also enjoy opportunities in cosmetics, textiles, food and drink, biotechnology, medicine, pharmaceuticals, electronic device fabrication, and environmental organizations.

Chemical engineers have also been active in meeting many of the world's environmental challenges. They develop technologies to monitor devices, modeling techniques, and operating strategies. They use their unique expertise to help them understand how to positively affect the environment. For example, they may work at reducing the volume and toxicity of pollutants in the air. Reducing the pollutants means that fewer toxins will enter waterways and topsoil. These efforts play a major role in reducing the negative environmental impact of industrial facilities, such as power plants and factories. A cleaner environment benefits everyone.

What They Can Do

If you become a chemical engineer, you will have many opportunities to do important things. With the opportunity to focus on health, safety, sustainability, nutrition, and even high-tech communication devices, chemical engineers can tackle a wide variety of important jobs, from developing medical tests or treatments for cancer patients to making more environmentally friendly household products. The possibilities are endless! Here are just a few industries where chemical engineers are making a difference.

FOOD SCIENCE

When we do our grocery shopping, we usually have a variety of safe and fresh foods to choose from. Or we can choose ready-to-eat foods, or products that are quick and easy to prepare. We can eat at restaurants with confidence that our meals are safe and free from contaminants. None of this would be possible without the work of chemical engineers. Thanks to them, there are sterilization procedures in place to protect against food illnesses such as salmonella and E. coli poisoning.

Chemical engineers also help with procedures related to spoilage, packaging, and shelf life. When plants are harvested, they begin to spoil right away. The chemical reactions that take place in a living plant continue to happen, but in a way that weakens the plant. It immediately starts to rot. The same thing happens with animal products, such as meat, eggs, and dairy.

Refrigeration is an excellent way to slow spoilage. The cooler temperatures slow the activity of the microorganisms in the product as well as the rates of some chemical reactions. Chemical engineers can help further by improving the packaging to reduce the amount of air getting to the product, especially since oxygen is highly reactive. The less oxygen in direct contact with our food the better.

COSMETICS

Chemical engineers working in the cosmetics industry develop products for personal care, such as cosmetics, sunscreens, lotions, and body creams. One problem they had to solve is keeping larger molecules in some substances from sinking. This process is called emulsion, and it's necessary to stabilize the products. Have you ever had to shake a can of paint before using it? The emulsion process ensures that particles stay suspended in the liquid paint and prevents the larger particles from settling.

In addition, chemical engineers have developed airless bottles and pumps, which are an important quality control to avoid microbial contamination during product manufacturing. Chemical engineers also monitor pH control and emulsion to ensure rigorous production processes to prevent the growth of potentially harmful microbes.

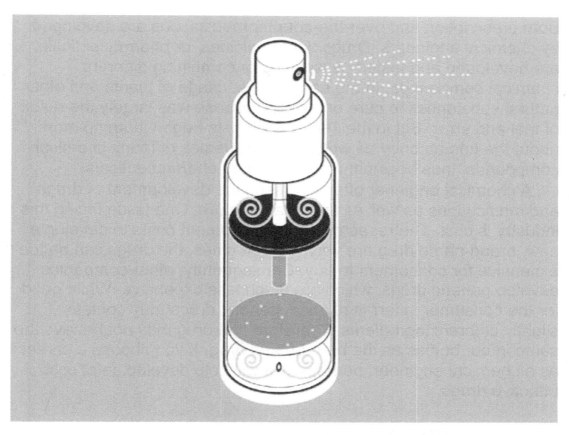

FIGURE 4: *Diagram of an airless pump*

Chemical engineers develop naturally derived, nontoxic, and cruelty-free alternatives to existing products to make cosmetics safer, more ethical, and better for the environment. For example, certain parabens are a class of chemicals that prevent bacterial growth. They are often used as preservatives in cosmetics as well as in food and drugs. There is evidence that parabens cause hormonal disruptions, so chemical engineers have found alternatives in response to the demand for paraben-free products.

PHARMACEUTICALS

Both prescription and over-the-counter medications are developed by chemical engineers. Drugs and medicines, or pharmaceuticals, are developed and tested by isolating or combining different chemical compounds. In the early 1800s, usage of plants and other natural substances to cure or prevent disease was largely the result of trial and error. But in the 1900s, scientists began learning more about the human body as well as the properties of many chemical compounds, thus beginning the science of pharmaceuticals.

A chemical engineer often oversees the development of drugs and medications as well as their manufacture. One issue facing this industry is cost. The research and development costs to develop a new, brand-name drug are very high. At times, the drugs can be too expensive for consumers to buy. Consequently, other companies develop generic drugs, which are much less expensive. While good for the consumer in terms of price, generic drugs may contain slightly different ingredients. Therefore, the drug may not behave the same in our bodies as the brand-name drug. If you choose a career as a chemical engineer, perhaps you will help develop safe, cost-effective drugs.

THE OIL AND GAS INDUSTRY

Our society is heavily dependent on the products produced by petroleum. We don't just use petroleum to produce oil and gas. Petroleum also forms the basis of plastics, preservatives used in our food, shampoo, and many more household products. Chemical engineers working in this field have an important job in ensuring that the mixtures to produce gasoline and other products are correct. They may work on oil rigs or on ships, or they may work in laboratories. One important area they concentrate on is reducing pollution by developing cleaner sources of energy.

PLASTICS

Plastic is everywhere: in our computers, handheld devices, kitchens, cars, food packaging, and even some of our clothing. Plastics are made from polymers, which are long, stable molecules made from the carbon atoms in fossil fuels. When plastics were first developed in the late 1800s, people used them instead of products made from other natural resources, so they were considered beneficial and a form of natural preservation. But now, plastics pose a huge problem because they take years to break down when tossed into the garbage. There are different opinions on how long the breakdown process takes, but the range is considered to be about 20 to 1,000 years, depending on the type of plastic.

Some chemical engineers working in the plastics industry are now focusing on this issue. They are considering ways to manufacture plastics in a form that is easier to break down. This would be accomplished through a recycling process. Another approach was recently taken by a Canadian high school student named Daniel Burd. Understanding that bacteria help break down organic material, Daniel entered—and won—a science fair in which he showed that two bacteria strains were able to break down a plastic. A team of scientists and engineers could work on this idea and develop a solution to our environmental problem. Perhaps you have an idea to investigate on how to solve this important issue! Students can make a difference.

ENERGY TECHNOLOGIES

Chemical engineers contribute to the development of various traditional energy sources, such as those involving fossil fuels. They are also active in developing and refining other nontraditional energy sources. For example, chemical engineers help formulate the types of durable plastics needed in wind turbines.

Another area in which chemical engineers contribute is the development of fuel cells. Fuel cells are a more efficient source of energy than combustion engines, and the only emission from a fuel cell is water, unlike emissions from combustion engines. Many buses, cars, and boats use fuel cell technology.

In a fuel cell, the chemical energy of the fuel is converted to usable energy, such as electrical energy. Briefly, a solution of methanol (a type of alcohol) and water sits on a plate of platinum. Here, the methanol molecules release some of their hydrogen atoms, which produces an electric current. The platinum is a catalyst; that is, the platinum helps the reaction take place. However, platinum is expensive. Currently, chemical engineers don't fully understand the chemistry of the catalyst reactions. However, chemical engineers at the University of Wisconsin—Madison have simulated various reactions on a computer and learned that the role of water is more important in fuel cell technology than previously thought. Their work could lead to less-expensive fuel cells.

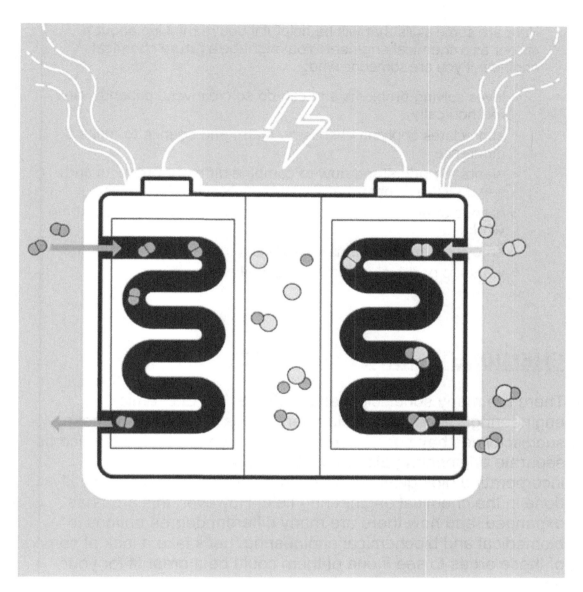

FIGURE 5: *Diagram of a fuel cell*

CAREER CHECKLIST

Here are some skills that will be helpful if you're thinking about a career as a chemical engineer. You might be a future chemical engineer if you are someone who:

- loves solving problems and can do so creatively, patiently, and methodically
- appreciates applying chemistry, math, and science to make a difference
- wants to understand how to combine different products and see how they work together
- is good at organizing problems and figuring out how something works
- enjoys solving problems involving biology
- wants to positively impact the global environment

CHEMICAL ENGINEERING SPECIALTIES

There are many subdisciplines within the field of chemical engineering. Since the development of this field, some of these subdisciplines have grown broader and even expanded to become separate engineering disciplines themselves. For example, incorporating biological principles into engineering was originally done in the chemical engineering field. However, this area has expanded, and now there are many different degree options in biomedical and biochemical engineering. Let's take a look at some of these areas to see if one of them could be a great fit for your goals.

Biomedical Engineering

A multidisciplinary field, biomedical engineering combines biology and engineering to apply engineering principles and materials science to medicine and health care. Biomedical engineers work on solving problems and creating advances that influence people directly and indirectly. For example, a biomedical engineer could help design prosthetic devices, such as artificial limbs.

Biomedical engineers develop solutions such as surgical devices and robotics or laser technologies to support surgical procedures, which helps doctors, nurses, and other medical professionals. They can also work closely with other engineers to develop innovative solutions that affect the world. In addition to designing external devices such as artificial limbs, biomedical engineers also develop systems to monitor vital information such as blood chemistry, oxygen levels, and body composition.

There is a growing need for new medical devices. As a biomedical engineer, you could wind up designing devices that allow people to monitor and control conditions such as diabetes, or maybe you could help design new pacemakers to manage heart activity. There may even be opportunities to design and produce artificial organs!

Biochemical Engineering

Biochemical engineering involves using natural or organic materials to develop products and processes. Do you have a favorite color of clothing? There's a good chance that a biochemical engineer worked with a team to generate that color. These engineers also ensure that the material coloring agents are safe. In addition to making clothing colorful, biochemical engineers develop chemicals that help preserve the shelf life of food, drinks, and even medications. They also identify ways in which oil, petroleum, and other fuels can be refined as gasoline to reduce pollution.

Another example of a biochemical engineer's job is ensuring that a community's water source is clean and safe for human consumption. This is especially important in some communities in which there is limited access to clean water. When people are forced to drink and bathe in dirty water, this can lead to disease and even death.

Environmental Engineering

Environmental engineering focuses on addressing current and emerging challenges to the environment, including the air, water, and land. This includes understanding how engineers can use chemicals, materials, and processes to promote a healthy environment. Chemical engineering has always been a major contributor to environmental protection. With a unique background, environmental engineers with a chemistry background work in teams with other professionals to address the complex problems and challenges facing the world today, for example, site cleanup and decontamination, water treatment, and pollution control.

One success in this area is the development of the reverse osmosis process. During reverse osmosis, contaminants are removed from drinking water. The water passes through a partially permeable membrane. The membrane acts as a screen and allows only certain particles (the contaminants) to pass through.

According to UNICEF, access to clean water and proper sanitation is a problem. Millions of people around the world do not have safe water or adequate sanitation, and many more are affected by the diseases that result from these inadequate conditions. Environmental engineers are involved in addressing many of the challenges associated with these unacceptable conditions. One solution they have devised is to use oxidizing agents in water that is unsafe to use. Oxidation is a chemical reaction that involves electrons going from one substance to another. The change in electrons changes the structure of the substances. In the case of microorganisms in water, the change in structure makes it easier to remove them. Using oxidation, environmental engineering ingenuity has resulted in a number of different techniques to purify our drinking water.

Some environmental engineers work with scientists and other engineers to design cost-effective devices that reduce the amount of pollution produced by cars and trucks. These engineers also look at fuel consumption, since improving a vehicle's fuel consumption can help reduce the emissions polluting the air. Then there's the fuel itself. Engineers improve the techniques to refine the raw materials that are used to make gasoline and petroleum. These improvements have significantly lowered the levels of pollutants such as sulfur emitted into our atmosphere.

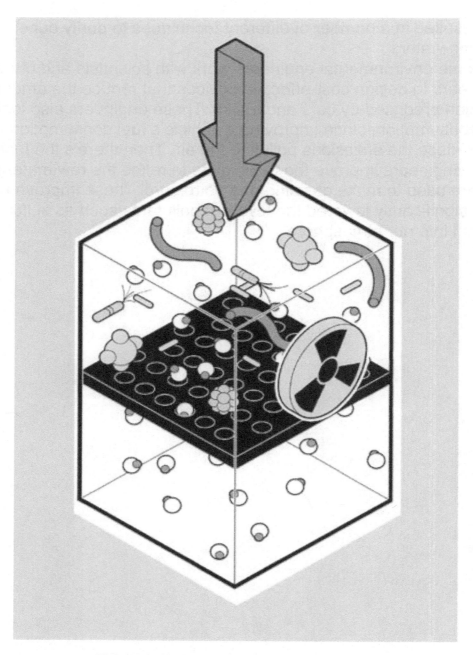

FIGURE 6: *Diagram of reverse osmosis*

Materials Engineering

Materials engineers study, develop, and test materials composed of a variety of substances. These engineers also investigate the properties and structures of various materials, such as plastics, metals, ceramics, and nanomaterials, evaluating them to see how they meet certain mechanical, chemical, and electrical requirements. The materials engineers may then be able to advance the material's performance in some way. A materials engineer might work on developing and testing materials used to create a variety of things, from computer chips and medical devices to basketballs and snowboards.

New materials have been among the most significant achievements of every era. They have been essential to the growth, prosperity, security, and quality of life for humans since the beginning of time. New materials have been critical in opening the door to innovations in areas such as civil, chemical, construction, aeronautical, and electrical engineering. Materials engineers continue to be at the forefront of these and many other areas as they understand how to design products and apply new materials for the development of innovative products.

The opportunities for impact as a materials engineer are broad. They range from clothing to sports-related applications to medical interventions. For example, materials engineers have developed materials to produce clothing that repels mosquitoes. Some medical applications in this field are nano-size polymers to repair fractured and shattered human bones. Biomedical applications of new materials include developing materials to support skin healing during skin grafting, a surgical procedure to help burn victims heal faster in which the doctor removes skin from one area of the body and transplants it to a different one.

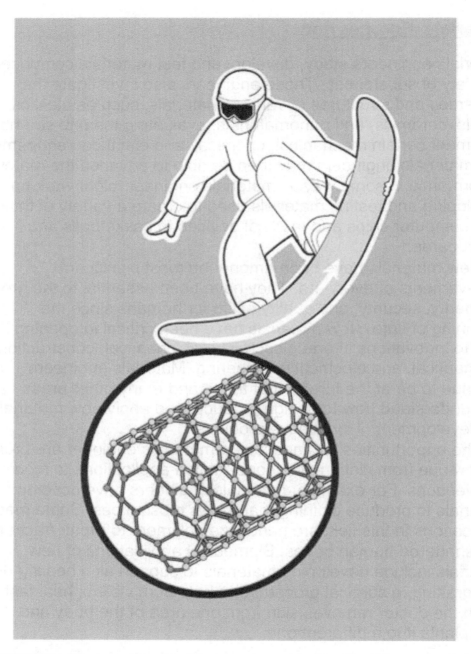

FIGURE 7: *Diagram of a flexible snowboard built with carbon nanotubes*

Nuclear Engineering

Nuclear engineers focus on safe, innovative, and efficient applications of nuclear energy. Nuclear energy is the energy available in the atom. The amount of energy released during a nuclear reaction is huge, so working with nuclear energy is very dangerous.

The use of nuclear energy could be in medical equipment, radioactive waste disposal facilities, or nuclear power plants. Nuclear engineers are heavily involved in the electrical power production industry. The United States gets about 20 percent of its electricity from nuclear power plants, according to the World Nuclear Association. Nuclear energy is generated in more than 430 nuclear power plants worldwide, with approximately 100 of these plants being in the United States.

Nuclear engineers work with medical professionals to develop safe processes using radioactive materials for diagnosis. This integration of nuclear engineering and medicine is called nuclear medicine. This branch of medicine uses radioactive tracers (radiopharmaceuticals) in the body to help diagnose and treat diseases. Doctors and technologists who administer these tests use cameras specially designed to track the tracers in a patient's body.

Nuclear energy can be very dangerous, so safety is important. Nuclear engineers work hard to keep communities and nations from risk while still providing much-needed electricity. If you become a nuclear engineer, you could work with nuclear energy as a medical application or a source of energy, as a consultant providing guidelines on how to handle and dispose of nuclear waste, or as an analyst looking at nuclear accidents.

CHALLENGES IN CHEMICAL ENGINEERING

Perhaps the greatest challenge facing chemical and other engineers today is climate change. One of the main objectives in combating climate change is reducing greenhouse gases, which cause the global temperature to increase. Even a very small increase in temperature, such as 2 degrees, is too much. A slightly warmer temperature means the planet is out of balance. The higher temperature means more icebergs and glaciers will melt. Glacier melt affects the availability of fresh water reaching rivers and streams. The overall melt means a rise in sea level, which will put many cities and communities underwater.

A slight increase in ocean and lake water temperature also destroys delicate ecosystems. If the water is only half a degree warmer, many species of plant and aquatic life cannot survive. This creates a domino effect: the food for larger fish is unavailable, so the fish die. With no fish, the birds die, and so on.

Greenhouse gases come from pollutants and emissions from vehicles, industry, and buildings. The worst emissions are from fossil fuels, such as gasoline and coal. One of their byproducts is carbon dioxide, which is a major greenhouse gas.

Many advancements have been made with vehicles, especially the introduction of electric and hybrid vehicles. Even energy management in buildings is improving, with renewable energy sources such as wind and solar. What about industry?

Industries continue to fine-tune their production processes, but their energy demands are still high. One problem is waste. For example, many metals industries use only a quarter of the steel and only half of the aluminum they buy. The rest is reused, but that means using more energy again and producing more emissions. In another example, associate MIT professor Elsa Olivetti is a materials engineer who has been bothered by industrial waste. She has developed a "biobrick" called the Eco-BLAC brick from by-products from pulp and paper plants, turning a waste product into a sustainable construction material.

Another problem, especially in the oil and gas industry, is another gas: methane. Methane is second only to carbon dioxide as a major greenhouse gas.

Chemical engineers can help industries reduce climate change by redesigning processes to use materials more efficiently. At the same time, they can consider introducing greener energy sources. This will eventually lead to fewer emissions, which means less greenhouse gas in the atmosphere.

LOOKING AHEAD

The broad application of chemical engineering knowledge means that there are many areas in which to specialize. In the next five to ten years, chemical engineers will be working on products that affect the health, well-being, and environmental safety of our society and societies around the world.

In medicine, chemical engineers will continue to develop materials to enhance healing of the human body and to make new organs. Chemical and bioengineers are working on, among other technologies, a blood test to detect cancer instead of having a doctor perform a surgery such as a biopsy. When a medical test such as this can replace surgery, life is easier and safer. Plus, a blood test is much more affordable than surgery.

In electronics, chemical engineers will be developing more nanotechnologies to support the development of smart devices. Consequently, chemical engineers will also need to learn new ways to safely dispose of waste associated with electronics. Currently, people do not always dispose of their electronics properly. Electronics use many hazardous materials, such as lead and mercury. They have to be disposed of properly so waste sites are not contaminated. In addition, many electronics use precious metals, such as gold and copper. There is a whole industry devoted to extracting valuable materials from electronics, but because of the harmful materials, the people working to extract the valuable materials can be put at risk.

Chemical engineers are also increasingly more involved in biological research. One important future direction of chemical engineering is understanding human organ physiology and pathology (the study of diseases). Another is figuring out how to use chemical engineering principles while working with biological scientists and bioengineers to develop replacement limbs and organs and solutions to heal human skin that will not be rejected by the human body. New chemical engineers working in biotechnology will need biology training.

Sophisticated computer modeling software is becoming more available. More and more chemical engineers and chemists are able to model any scenarios they wish. They can work at a computer instead of in a lab to test a chemical reaction and see whether their predictions regarding results, rates of reaction, and product development are correct. This approach may prove helpful if they are working on a dangerous technique or using toxic materials. They can then analyze their results and apply their knowledge to the technology they are developing.

The field of chemical engineering is changing so quickly. To be successful, we need to adapt to society and understand technology as it evolves, especially with new materials opportunities and computing technologies. Those in the chemical engineering field will need to continue to develop their knowledge and work collaboratively with individuals in biology, mechanical engineering, electrical engineering, and other disciplines to develop the innovations needed for the future and to help protect the environment.

What's the most rewarding part about being an engineer?

"Engineers are changing the world in amazing ways and I like that an engineering degree is really a problem-solving degree, so that no matter what you end up doing with your degree, you will be a good problem solver—and that is a valuable skill to have in all walks of life."

—RACHEL BORRELLI, *materials science engineer*

Work in Progress

Manufacturing human organs used to be the stuff of science fiction movies and novels, but chemical engineering is making it a reality.

At the Wyss Institute at Harvard University, scientists and engineers have developed a procedure to make an artificial heart using human cells. This procedure, called tissue engineering, is still very new and needs to be tested before it is available to use in people waiting for a heart transplant.

The tissue needed for the new heart is grown in a laboratory. It acts just like a human heart—it beats, just like our own hearts beat.

The scientists have also carved tiny blood vessels that will activate once the heart has been transplanted. The technique is called SWIFT, which stands for "sacrificial writing into functional tissue." The process is a type of 3D printing, only the engineers use human tissue to "print" the organ. The original tissue is taken from the person who needs a new heart. Using the transplant recipient's own tissue helps reduce the chance of the body rejecting the new heart.

The tissue used contains stem cells. Stem cells are cells that haven't developed into specialized cells yet. For instance, there are muscle cells, brain cells, skin cells, and so on. Scientists call stem cells "undifferentiated." Imagine a piece of modeling clay: it's just a ball of clay until you decide what to make. Stem cells can be likened to the modeling clay: the cells can be "instructed" to specialize, or develop, into the type of cell needed, in this case heart cells.

If SWIFT is successful, scientists are optimistic that the procedure can be used to generate other organs, such as kidneys and livers. The waiting lists for organ donations can be quite lengthy. Another application is a "bio-band aid" to help burn victims grow new skin. Many lives could be saved or improved by having the ability to use 3D bio-printing. Innovative and creative thinking like this can have a powerful, positive effect on the health and welfare of people.

While organ manufacturing is still a work in progress, similar developments in the medical field have been successful. The world's first 3D printed tibia (shin bone) has been transplanted into the shin of an Australian man who was facing leg amputation.

To get the exact shape and detail of the tibia, engineers used an image of the original bone, which was obtained by an MRI (magnetic resonance image) of the patient. The 3D-printed tibia from the Australian man was wrapped in blood vessels and collagen tissue from both of his legs and implanted in a series of five surgeries. Engineering contributions are at the center of this medical achievement, officially declared a success, that many would have called impossible just a few short years ago.

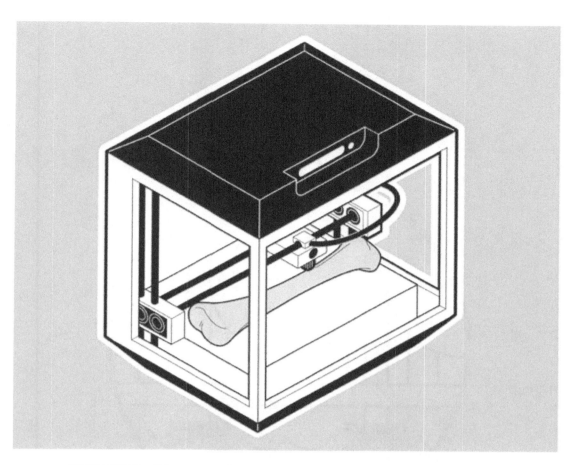

FIGURE 8: *Diagram of a 3D printer that is printing a tibia bone*

Chapter 3
CIVIL ENGINEERING

INSPIRING INNOVATION

Recently, the city of San Diego, California, found itself in need of an updated water treatment plant. The oldest of its three existing facilities, the Earl Thomas Reservoir, was built in the 1950s. After more than 50 years of use, it became clear that the plant was in need of a redesign. It needed modernization updates, and it was unlikely that the facility could withstand an earthquake. With the Rose Canyon Fault running through San Diego County and the San Andreas Fault running up and down the state of California, the city needed to find a safe and sustainable solution.

The renovated Alvarado Water Treatment Plant more than doubles San Diego's water filtration capacity and incorporates new technologies. The site also houses the offices and labs for the chemists who test the water from the other two treatment plants in San Diego, as well as the ocean water in the nearby Pacific.

The expansion project was massive. Two new water storage tanks had to be built, each one with a capacity of about 20 million gallons. Then the water treatment processes had to change. The old plant was using chlorine to disinfect the water. Chlorine does a good job of destroying bacteria in water, but while chlorine dissolves well in water, it does leave a taste. The California Department of Health Services upgraded the treatment processes, so the plant had to be changed. Instead of using chlorine, the plant now uses ozone to treat the water. Ozone has been proven to be more effective than chlorine in destroying bacteria, and it does not leave a taste, so the water tastes better. Ozone also helps reduce unwanted metals in water, such as sulfur and iron. The facility now has a large, new building to contain the system needed to generate the ozone.

The developers also supplemented the plant's energy source with solar energy to help run it. The Alvarado Water Treatment Plant has more than 6,000 solar panels on top of each storage tank. The addition of solar energy reduces the yearly electricity bill by about $40,000.

Engineers also worked to make the facility safer if an earthquake strikes by placing rubber pads between the roof and walls as well as between the floor and walls. There are also cables to allow for any shaking caused by an earthquake.

Other changes to the plant include filter and pipe upgrades, new tanks added to hold other treatment chemicals, a new water supply tank, and new tunnels linking the storage tanks.

The project was so large and complex that the American Society of Civil Engineers awarded the Alvarado Water Treatment Plant the Outstanding Civil Engineering Achievement Award in 2013.

What advice would you give to someone who's thinking about becoming an engineer?

"Do it because you want to help people and improve the community. Always keep learning and evolving. Engineering should never stay stagnant."

—**LEONARD TATE**, *engineering consultant specializing in water infiltration and remediation*

DEEP DIVE

Civil engineers design and build various structures, such as roads, bridges, airports, and energy and water systems to help protect the environment. During a project, they work with the contractors hired to do the work as well as the customer paying for the work. Civil engineers are also involved in the maintenance of everything they design.

Considered the first engineering discipline, civil engineering dates as far back as ancient Egypt. At that time, engineers devised ways to design and build impressive structures such as the Great Pyramid of Giza. Pyramid builders cut and moved more than two million blocks of stone and then went on to build the nearly 500-foot-high structure over the course of 20 years. Today, the only things that have changed in the field of civil engineering are technologies, materials, processes, and the outcome of what is designed.

In addition to designing roads and bridges, civil engineers have saved millions of lives through innovative technologies. They find solutions to protect structures used to contain liquids and nonhazardous substances, such as solid waste. They can also be used to contain hazardous substances, so they don't leak into the ground or water. Civil engineers have also made a tremendous impact on traffic control and road safety.

As a civil engineer, you could wind up working with a team to design and plan construction projects. This also involves predicting the long-term effects of the structures, systems, and materials, so understanding the environment of the structure's location is also important. Civil engineers need to have a solid understanding of conditions that affect structures, such as properties of various materials, stress, and thermodynamics.

Before construction on a project begins, civil engineers are involved in investigating everything related to the project and the site: the design, the environment, the site itself, the materials, and the projected costs. Civil engineers need strong organizational and analytical skills to estimate costs, make budgets, and plan for the future maintenance costs of a project. They may also be required to make presentations in front of government officials or company leaders to convey the details of the project and answer questions.

What They Can Do

Civil engineers have the opportunity to help people, communities, and societies in a variety of ways. As a civil engineer, you could focus on sustainability, ecology, disaster preparedness and relief, or even agriculture. Here are just a few areas where civil engineers have the opportunity to make a difference.

FLOOD CONTROL

Flooding can be traumatic to a community, most obviously in terms of loss of life and property damage. In the United States, more than 100 people lose their lives to floods every year. This number is expected to rise as climate change worsens. Repairs to bridges, roads, and other structures as a result of flooding cost almost $50 billion during the period between 1998 and 2014. Flooding can also lead to environmental erosion.

Some innovative civil and environmental engineers are tasked with devising solutions to help reduce flooding. One group of engineers at a company called Tarmac have developed a product called Topmix Permeable. Topmix is concrete, but it has holes. When the rain hits the concrete, the water flows through the holes. In one minute, about 880 gallons of water can flow through this new concrete. Once the water flows through the layers, it is collected in pipes, which drain the water. Since the water doesn't sit in place, the flooding risk is eliminated.

One of the most valuable resources in the world is water. Civil engineers who develop innovative products that support better urban planning, create environmentally friendly parks, and help the environment significantly influence the quality of life for the world and are needed now more than ever before.

ALTERNATIVE HOUSING

For some, the answer to flooding and other natural disasters is the floating home. Civil engineers work with architects and urban planners to develop and build this up-and-coming type of home.

Floating homes are of interest for a few reasons. First and foremost, they are designed to last on water. With the challenges of climate change and rising sea levels, many homes and communities along coastlines are in danger. Having a home that can survive on water will most likely save a home from destructive flooding. In some places, hurricanes ravage the coastlines as well as areas that are farther inland. Floating-home designers and civil engineers have developed new technologies that allow a home to detect the change in water level, as during a powerful storm, and then raise the home to protect it.

Floating homes can also be eco-friendly. Engineers can design them to be self-sufficient, powered by solar energy and using fresh water accumulated during storms. There is also the benefit of not building a foundation deep in the ground and possibly disrupting the related ecosystems. However, some people are concerned about the effect of a floating home on the water ecosystem. Civil engineers must take that into consideration as well.

In Denmark, one company has designed some inexpensive student housing on the water. The engineers are using shipping containers that are no longer in use, so there is a recycling benefit as well. They are small, clean, and efficient and make use of shared access to bike racks and boat facilities.

What's the most rewarding part about being an engineer?

"Finding the 'best' solution for the problem. The 'a-ha!' moment!"

—**DR. ELENA NIRLO,** *civil engineer*

EARTHQUAKE-RESISTANT BUILDING DESIGN

In 2010, a powerful earthquake hit the nation of Haiti on the island of Hispaniola. Infrastructure there had not been constructed to withstand a magnitude 7.0 earthquake, so buildings in the cities and towns affected by the earthquake collapsed. About a million people —roughly one-third of the country's population—were left homeless. Thousands more died.

Building codes related to having earthquake-resistant structures are dependent on the location; an area's building codes must address the largest earthquake likely to happen there. In the case of the 2010 Haitian earthquake, there weren't any enforced building codes.

Earthquake-resistant structures can feature a variety of designs and materials. The structure has to be able to shake, or move back and forth, without falling apart during an earthquake. Many structures use concrete to make them solid, but that is too brittle; the buildings just crumble with the shaking motion of the ground. Engineers must consider all the materials used, such as supports and joints, to make sure they don't hinder the ability to shake. Today, concrete structures incorporate steel rods to make the building able to sway more.

Civil engineers specializing in this area have access to a lot of data and experience from how other countries have designed and built earthquake-resistant structures. Computer simulations are useful to the engineer in this field as well.

AGRICULTURE

According to the US Department of Agriculture, the world population will exceed 9 billion by 2050. In addition, more than 60 percent of people will live in urban areas, where access to fresh produce has been traditionally limited. There is also a problem with the availability of land suitable for farming—there is less of it now, thanks to urbanization and erosion. One way to help ensure that there is enough fresh food available for this growing population is vertical agriculture. Vertical agriculture can help meet the growing food demands of this large urban population in a way that is environmentally sustainable, conserves water, and reduces runoff.

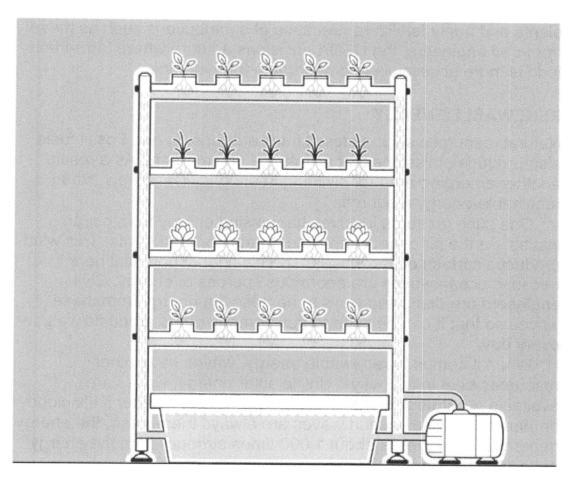

FIGURE 9: *Diagram of vertical farming*

This method of farming has plants growing on vertical structures, indoors, instead of the traditional outdoor farm on large plots of land. There are different advantages to this method. Farmers use LED lights instead of depending on sunlight. Studies have also shown that vertical farms use 70 percent less fertilizer and about 98 percent less water than traditional farming methods.

Civil engineers can help innovate and grow the vertical farming industry by designing the structures that hold the plants. They can also help design and develop systems to automatically water the plants and apply fertilizers. Because of contributions such as these from civil engineers, the USDA envisions a future where farm-fresh food is more accessible and affordable for everyone.

RENEWABLE ENERGY

Natural resources such as fossil fuels are running out. Fossil fuels also produce emissions that pollute the environment. As a result, another emerging area for civil engineering is finding new, clean renewable-energy resources.

One such resource involves harnessing energy from ocean waves. As the air over ocean water heats up, wind forms. This wind produces surface ocean waves. There's a lot of potential here because ocean waves are enormous sources of energy. Civil engineers are designing ways to harness the energy from these waves so that it can be used to power many of the products we use every day.

When it comes to renewable energy, waves have other resources beat in two ways. Unlike solar energy, waves are available regardless of the time of day. It doesn't matter if it's cloudy or there is no wind. Ocean waves are always there. Also, the energy generated by waves is about 1,000 times stronger than the energy generated by wind.

There are different ways to harness this energy. Some systems use the energy of the waves as they hit the shore. Other systems use the energy in waves far out in the ocean, or swells. Still others use the differences in water heights at low and high tides. But all systems lead to the same goal: converting the motion of the water to electrical energy. The electrical energy is then transformed into electricity, which is sent to our homes and businesses.

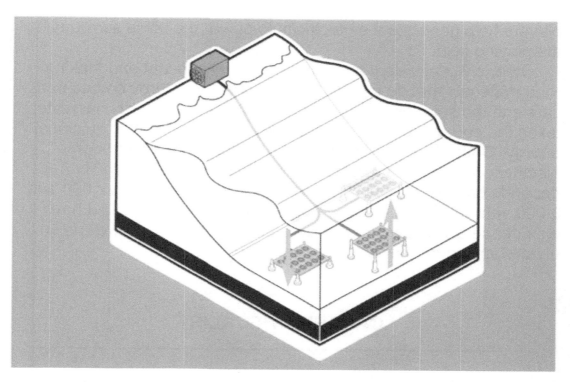

FIGURE 10: *Diagram of wave energy converting to electrical energy*

There are also new technologies being developed by civil engineers that use kinetic energy, the energy from motion. A person's or an object's kinetic energy is determined from its mass and speed. For instance, you have more kinetic energy when you are running than when you are walking.

One way civil engineers are harnessing kinetic energy is from people walking. They have developed a material—a type of tile—that takes the energy from feet hitting the ground and converts it to electrical energy. The electrical energy is then used to power electronic devices and lights. This material of course works best in areas where there are lots of pedestrians. One successful instance of this technology in action is in Rio de Janeiro, Brazil, where soccer players help generate the electricity to power the lights surrounding the playing field.

Other civil engineers are using the same concept and making road materials that do the same thing, only the energy comes from cars and the solar energy that hits the roads. An "energy harvester" takes the energy from moving vehicles and converts it to electrical energy. One example in the United Kingdom projects enough electricity to power between 2,000 and 4,000 streetlights. This depends on normal traffic for the area, which is between 2,000 and 3,000 vehicles per hour. Civil engineers working in this field have experience and knowledge in materials engineering as well as an understanding of energy technologies.

CAREER CHECKLIST

Civil engineering is a growing and varied field. There are a number of skills that lend themselves to being a civil engineer, including:

- being super-organized with a flair for planning and design
- a love for math and science, especially trigonometry and other advanced math topics that help you visualize outcomes
- strong written and verbal communication skills
- leadership skills
- technical skills, especially computer-aided design
- a knack for negotiating with others to meet project goals

CIVIL ENGINEERING SPECIALTIES

Civil engineers contribute to many areas; therefore, there are several subdisciplines. Many of these subdisciplines have grown to be unique and distinct engineering disciplines, but they are still very much related to the field of civil engineering. Many require you to be out of the office at different sites. Here are just some of the fields available.

Construction Engineering

There are many parts to working on a construction project. In addition to planning, designing, and maintaining buildings and other structures, construction engineers are also involved in project management, so they deal with people in every aspect of the project. There are other engineers to consult with, as well as the client and all the different contractors on the job, such as mechanics, electricians, and carpenters, so good communication skills are important. The construction engineer in charge also has to be well organized in order to manage schedules, hire the right contractors for the job, choose the right materials, and even help choose which equipment to use. Having surveying and sketching skills is also desirable.

Civil engineers who specialize in construction engineering work individually and in teams to plan, direct, and supervise various construction projects. Construction engineers also work on the design, development, and maintenance of large mechanical or electrical systems. They might also spend their day developing construction plans, overseeing engineering processes, managing construction projects, or drafting technical support documents. While some construction engineers spend the day in an office, it is not unusual for them to spend a lot of time on-site as well.

As with all engineering disciplines, a construction engineer can specialize in a specific industry, such as in aviation or energy. Many construction engineers will specialize in, say, residential or commercial buildings. Others may choose working on infrastructure systems, such as bridges, tunnels, and highways. There are also plenty of opportunities in the private sector designing and building stadiums and sports venues.

Environmental Engineering

Environmental engineers are concerned with protecting the environment and people from the adverse effects of pollution as well as improving overall environmental quality. They are educated in various sciences, such as biology, chemistry, physics, and geology. Like construction engineers, environmental engineers usually specialize in one area, such as air quality control, waste management, or water quality.

They design systems for waste management, devise site cleanup and contamination procedures, establish waste-treatment and pollution-control practices, and evaluate and enhance technology to protect the environment and resources. Such protection also helps prevent contaminants from getting into the water in people's homes. Environmental engineers are often called upon to advise different companies and different levels of government on various environmental concerns. For example, they may find ways to improve environmental protection and suggest how to proceed in cleaning up a toxic site.

An environmental engineer may work for the government, such as in a health department or an environmental agency. There are also opportunities in the private sector, such as with an engineering consulting firm or a utility company.

Outdoor work is an important part of this career choice. An environmental engineer has to visit sites, inspect them, take soil or water samples for analysis, and consult with company owners.

Back in the office, there is a lot of desk work involved, such as attending meetings, participating in phone calls, researching policies, collaborating with other professionals, writing reports, preparing materials for the government, preparing plans and models, attending meetings, and writing impact studies. An environmental engineer uses computer simulations to model systems for the project in order to analyze the project from a variety of perspectives to ensure safety.

Geotechnical Engineering

Geotechnical, or geological, engineers concentrate on soil and rock behavior. They want to understand how these natural environments affect the stability and slope of different land masses. This would be important, for example, if a township wanted to build a new road through an undeveloped area.

Geotechnical engineers also design systems to support and manage natural resources. A geotechnical engineer might design reservoirs for water treatment facilities, design and identify ideal locations for retaining walls, construct landfills and dams, or determine the slope for ground stability to assess the risk for natural disasters, such as landslides, sinkholes, avalanches, and earthquakes.

Geotechnical engineers are especially important to infrastructure development. During bridge construction, a geotechnical engineer would be called upon to assess the ground where the bridge supports are to be positioned. The material in the ground has to be able to hold up these supports. A geotechnical engineer would also be involved in designing tunnels going through rock. There are different challenges in this type of project. There is the rock itself that has to be understood, but there are also the effects of blasting the rock—stress and pressures can change the stability of the rock, potentially endangering workers. Building tunnels requires highly specialized geological knowledge as well as specialized equipment.

Daily activities for these engineers might include using tools for evaluation or designing multiple large structures in a city, park, or rural community. Boston's "Big Dig" is an example of a well-known geotechnical engineering project. The "Big Dig" replaced a 40-year-old interstate with a modern underground expressway. This traffic makeover required an innovative soil stabilization program due to poor soil conditions in the original structure. Engineers were also challenged to avoid interfering with regular downtown traffic as much as possible during the construction of the new tunnel system.

Municipal Engineering

Have you ever wondered how cities are planned? If the thought of developing a municipality or an urban community while keeping quality of life and environmental sustainability top-of-mind appeals to you, municipal engineering might be a good fit for you.

There is a great deal of research and planning that goes into developing a municipality. Just think of all the facilities in a town: water supply systems, water treatment systems, waste management, waste disposal, roads, public transportation, bridges, airports, train stations, business areas, residential areas, utilities such as electricity and gas, and public parks. These engineers are strongly engaged in the design of new communities and have a direct impact on the quality of life for the citizens in the places they are designing. They are also involved in maintaining and updating the structures, especially as new technologies emerge, such as those used to make smart cities. Municipal and urban engineers are employed by different municipalities.

Projects such as these can be large and complex, so a municipal engineer should have strong organizational, communication, and management skills. There are different teams to organize and manage, depending on the aspects of the project. A municipal engineer has to plan and organize the various work schedules and budgets. Once the project is underway, the engineer has to monitor everything. The municipal engineer must also be familiar with all sorts of regulations and building and industry codes so they can be sure the codes are enforced.

Municipal engineers work with a team of other professionals, including other engineers, city planners, architects, and landscape architects. Similar to all the other engineering disciplines, there are always reports to write as well as analyses and feasibility studies to undertake.

Transportation Engineering

As the name suggests, a transportation engineer designs and maintains a community's transportation routes and systems, including roads, bus infrastructure, subways, and train lines that run within and outside a city. Whatever the type of transportation, a transportation engineer ensures that the ride is safe, efficient, and comfortable for everyone. This includes understanding the best routes for public transportation, understanding how ride-share programs affect traffic flow, and allowing for emergency response by the fire department and emergency medical services. This might involve technology, for example, so that an emergency vehicle has a control to change a red light to a green light when it is safe to do so. Usually transportation engineering deals with land-based transportation, although it can also include developments and planning related to airports and seaports.

Today, with the importance of protecting our environment, there is more interest in planning for public transportation, since that has less impact on the environment. Some people want to use their cars less to cut down on emissions. Depending on the region, this could mean expanded public transportation that is efficient, cost-effective, and environmentally sustainable.

A transportation engineer could work for the government, especially with anything related to roads and other public uses. There are opportunities to work for private companies as well, such as being a consultant for a railroad or airline.

A transportation engineer needs to be able to analyze complex projects, such as monitoring traffic flow over a given area. They need to be able to propose safe and cost-effective solutions. Good communication skills are also required because transportation engineers need to be able to manage people and write reports.

CHALLENGES IN CIVIL ENGINEERING

In addition to upgrading existing physical infrastructures and maintaining communications infrastructures, new environmental challenges are surfacing for civil engineers. One in particular is related to climate change. As Earth's temperature rises, more and more glaciers and icebergs are melting. The additional water is causing sea levels to rise. There are many communities on shorelines around the world that are affected by rising sea levels. For example, New Orleans is sinking. When the city was built in the early 1700s, it was about 10 feet above sea level. Today, much of the city is below sea level, and it is expected to be 15 to 18 feet below sea level by the end of this century.

Other challenges include responding to disasters such as hurricanes and soil erosion, which can damage and even destroy buildings. The impact civil engineers will have on the future of society is significant.

Civil engineers spend considerable time addressing challenges related to water. Many communities do not have access to clean water. One clever solution to help with this problem involves the prickly pear cactus. Dr. Norma Alcantar, a professor at the University of South Florida in Tampa, had done research with the prickly pear cactus demonstrating that the plant's mucilage can be used to clean contaminated water. (Mucilage is a gelatin-like substance found in some plants.) She and her team had been working with this method before the Haiti earthquake in 2010. When the drinking water in Haiti became contaminated as a result of the earthquake, Dr. Alcantar learned that there were prickly pear cacti in Haiti, and she and her team began using their mucilage to purify water there.

Another coming challenge is the self-driving vehicle. Many automobile manufacturers are planning to have autonomous vehicles in production before 2030. While this will create an entirely new area of specialization for civil and transportation engineers, it will also create new challenges. For example, there will be new issues related to roadway safety, managing "mixed traffic" (traffic that includes self-driving and traditional vehicles), traffic management, signal communication, and roadway design.

LOOKING AHEAD

An emerging area of opportunity for civil engineers is designing landfills and waste disposal processes. Technology is always changing, so new systems are needed for new technologies. Civil engineers will be strongly engaged in understanding what types of landfills and disposal processes are appropriate. Some sites, for example, may have metals or other contaminants, so civil engineers need to take that into consideration. They will want to ensure that there is minimal impact on the environment and people living in the area. Additional areas of growth and opportunity are managing groundwater, reducing traffic congestion, improving building energy efficiency, and developing techniques to reduce the impact of soil erosion.

Homes, businesses, and now cities are becoming "smart." That is, more and more utilities and functions can be controlled from a remote location or by responding to a set of conditions. For example, you can control your lights at home while on vacation elsewhere if you have a smart system. Now apply that concept to a city and the multiple activities and services provided by a city. Civil engineers need to be aware of this trend toward "cities of the future" and help make it a reality.

It is probably easiest to build a smart city from scratch instead of trying to convert all the existing infrastructure to use smart technologies. This is happening in South Korea, where planners are building Songdo International Business District, the first smart city. It will have in place all the technology necessary to help and protect its citizens, for example, cameras. There will also be access to social media and sensors that will allow for feedback so citizens can make decisions based on that information.

One example is improving traffic congestion. The central system in Songdo monitors all the traffic systems. If a certain route is becoming too busy and congested, messages can be sent directly to buses on that route. If necessary, it can be changed to a more efficient and less congested route, or the number of buses on the route can be reduced. Saving the passengers time and keeping them happy are the goals.

This is exciting, and there may be multiple smart cities throughout the world one day. However, it's not likely that all existing cities will be converted to smart cities. Civil engineers will have to learn how to integrate smart technologies, infrastructure, and materials in the cities of today as well as design communication between smart cities and traditional communities.

An enduring opportunity for civil and structural engineers is the development of innovative processes, materials, and designs to facilitate electronic communication. Strong and creative engineering minds will be needed in the telecommunications industry for many decades to come to provide services, from cell tower design and analysis, to modification of the design of existing structures, to the examination of potential areas for locating these towers.

FIGURE 11: *Diagram of a smart city*

Work in Progress

The research and development efforts of civil engineers are impacting many current and future designs and processes. One ongoing research project is looking, again, at water. In many communities in the United States, we tend to overuse water. Engineers are researching economical devices to recycle water rather than throwing it away.

We have talked a lot about water in this book, but it's one of the most precious resources on the planet. We need it for virtually every aspect of our lives. We have an abundance of water in many parts of the United States, but many communities both here and abroad do not have access to good-quality water. In other parts of the world, some communities do not have access to water at all. The ability of engineers to address this problem will improve the quality of life for many people around the world.

We have access to so much ocean water, but drinking seawater is not an option. We can't irrigate our crops with salty water, either. Too much salt is toxic for most plants.

A new project led by the Lawrence Berkeley National Laboratory in California is researching ways to desalinate, or remove the salt from, seawater, as well as removing any contaminants in it. If successful, the new process may provide drinking water as well as water for crops. With successful decontamination, this could be an alternative for cleaning industrial wastewater and even sewage. The Berkeley project team has an ambitious goal to develop the technologies to enable 90 percent of nontraditional water sources to be reused at the same cost as traditional water sources.

This project requires completely different thinking for the team of civil engineers supporting this effort. Today, our water systems use a straightforward method, or linear delivery. This means extracting fresh water, treating it, using treated wastewater, and disposing of it. This has been a good system. However, the increasing population is proving to be a strain on linear delivery, and new approaches are needed. The project from Berkeley will access water sources that may contain salt or contaminants from various production facilities or a salty underwater source. The water will then be treated with Berkeley's innovative purification technologies and transformed into clean, safe, usable water. By recycling the water, the method becomes a circular system instead of a linear one. So being creative and thinking outside the box are definite assets to this career choice. What a way to change the world!

FIGURE 12: *Diagram of the Berkeley project*

Chapter 4
ELECTRICAL ENGINEERING

INSPIRING INNOVATION

In June 2019, the UN Convention on the Rights of Persons with Disabilities recognized that artificial intelligence (AI) has the potential to enhance inclusion, participation, and independence for people with disabilities. AI is the use of computers to think for us, do tasks, and adapt those tasks when necessary. AI is already an established field, with many of our technologies using it. For example, when we check our email, the tools that catch our spelling and sometimes grammar errors use AI and "natural language processing," which is how computer programmers describe the interpretation by computers of our everyday language. And when we do a computer search? Those ads that always appear are based on AI algorithms; they're tailored to the search history of the person doing the searching. Here are just a few more technologies present in our everyday lives that use AI algorithms: the personal assistants in our cell phones and homes, self-driving cars, autonomous appliances such as vacuum cleaners, thermostats that can predict your preferred temperature at home, and medical applications.

AI holds tremendous potential for helping people with vision, hearing, mobility, and cognitive and learning disabilities enjoy a better quality of life. AI-powered assistive technologies have been shown to offer significant benefits for people with disabilities, especially in the areas of human connection, education, and employment. All this is possible when engineers apply "inclusive design" to AI solutions. Inclusive design means designing something that as many people as possible can use.

Approximately 70 million people who are hearing impaired use sign language as a first language for communication. An example of an innovative technology that electrical engineers are working on that supports this segment of the population is called "sign to text." Not everyone knows or uses sign language, so "sign to text" helps people with a hearing impairment communicate effectively. They record their hand movements on a device like a tablet. Then the device converts the signs into voice or text. The device includes a 3D camera to track the signer's movements, making it possible for individuals with a hearing impairment to communicate with anyone.

One pioneer of this technology, a company called KinTrans, has already begun applying machine-learning algorithms to gather the necessary data to teach its AI program to process sign language data inputs from a 3D camera and convert it to text. This type of programing requires a massive amount of training data, which is currently being collected to build a robust 3D database of American Sign Language body movements.

FIGURE 13: *Diagram of "sign to text"*

A team of students at the University of Pittsburgh is also using computer engineering in a similar way, but these students wanted to do so with smaller data sets, which means faster translation. Students Christopher Pasquinelli and Haihui Zhu started with American Sign Language and translating to text. Because of the vast amount of data generated, the team reduced the information that had to be processed by designating 23 key points on the hand. The system tracks these 23 points and then a computer algorithm translates the movements into text.

DEEP DIVE

Electrical engineering is one of the newer branches of engineering and deals with the technology of electricity. Electrical engineers work specifically with systems using electronics, electricity, telecommunications, signal processing, and electromagnetism. An electrical engineer applies the math and physics of electrical energy and electricity and develops new systems and equipment to benefit society and solve problems. Electrical engineers have many opportunities to work in the private sector, government, major research institutions, and national labs, focusing on areas such as energy efficiency, mobile technology, accessibility, transportation, telecommunications, Global Positioning System (GPS), Internet accessibility, and more.

Since the nineteenth century, electrical engineering has been at the forefront of innovation. From the tiny microchip to the massive power station, the impact of electrical and computer engineering and computer science can be seen in nearly every aspect of our lives. Some of the most prominent engineers in history have been electrical engineering pioneers, including Thomas Edison, inventor of the light bulb; Guglielmo Marconi, credited as the inventor of radio; and Philo Farnsworth, inventor of the television.

Over the years, the electrical engineering field has influenced societies and cultures across the country and around the world.

Electrical engineers have produced many groundbreaking innovations that we take for granted. The introduction of cell phones and computers has made communication so much easier, increasing the spread of ideas throughout the world. People can now interact, share, and obtain medical services, access to education, and other needed resources without physical contact or the expense of traveling. And consider the Internet: While it's been in development for more than 50 years, electrical engineers have put its development and accessibility at a global level. As a result, individuals are able to connect and communicate around the world as well as enhance safety through tracking systems, promote healthy crop development, and improve education and access to knowledge to help those in more remote communities live better.

Electrical engineers' work also encompasses medical technology, such as MRI scanners, lab equipment, dialysis machines, and pacemakers and other implantable electronics. Electrical engineers might work alongside mechanical engineers in developing assistive devices like surgical robots, working on the hardware and software development.

What They Can Do

Work done by electrical engineers touches so many aspects of our lives. Using our ovens, lighting our homes, and powering up our computers cannot be done without electrical engineers. But electrical engineers shape the more extraordinary elements in our lives, too. Here are just a few industries in which electrical engineers are making a difference.

HEALTH AND SAFETY

If you've ever used an app with GPS to navigate to a mapped address or find a lost phone, you can thank an electrical engineer for those systems. GPS has been especially important in increasing driver safety and reducing the risk of accidents. For example, many people drive for a living: truck drivers, ride-share and taxi drivers, and delivery drivers. Not only does GPS help drivers get to their destination, but a GPS safety tracking component can keep the drivers from distracted driving. When people do something other than drive, such as eat, text, or hold a cell phone to their ear, they are distracted. The GPS safety tracking component will prevent a call or text from coming through while the person is driving. The person sending the message receives an auto reply saying the driver is unavailable.

Companies have designed products with GPS technology incorporated in bracelets or placed in backpacks and purses. This tracking technology is being used to help track individuals, find children, and locate adults with diseases such as Alzheimer's disease. In fact, one company has developed a tennis shoe with built-in GPS tracking for people with Alzheimer's. The shoe is called the GPS SmartSole. People with Alzheimer's have memory and orientation problems and get confused easily. They aren't supposed to go out by themselves, but it happens sometimes. When it does, they cannot always remember to take a cell phone or tracking device with them, and then they may get lost and not understand what to do next. With this new technology, as long as the person goes out with the shoes on, they are traceable.

AGRICULTURE

Farmers routinely use satellite images to assess their fields and ensure acres of land are developing properly. This, too, is the work of electrical engineering. Electrical engineers helped develop the satellites as well as the electronics and sensors used.

When satellite technology first became more available to nonmilitary users, farmers used it to see how much farmland was being used. Now, farmers use data from satellites in a variety of ways. It is common for farmers to have access to new satellite images every week.

Some satellites monitor for irrigation needs, so farmers know from the image which areas need more water instead of manually inspecting the farmland. Large farms may have acres and acres of crops, so having to walk the fields or even drive through them is very time-consuming.

Some satellite images can identify crop type and help farmers understand when the crops will be ready to harvest. This helps the farmer organize the labor needed to help harvest. This information is also useful for estimating when certain crops will be ready to ship out to food distributors.

Satellite data can also detect whether any crops are being affected by pests. This is another time-saving aid for farmers because they don't have to walk the fields to find out this information. This way, they know in advance where to add more pesticides. Farmer can also see from the images where more fertilizer needs to be added.

And, as with almost all technologies today, farmers can use smart technology and monitor their crops from their phones.

EDUCATION

Anyone with an Internet connection has access to millions of terabytes of data and information. People who lived just a century ago had no such access to information. You have access to the largest public library with just a few clicks of the mouse, all thanks to the electrical engineers of the 1960s and 1970s who developed the Internet. Electrical engineers were responsible for introducing the Transmission Control Protocol, or TCP, in 1981. TCP is used for most of the Internet. And in 2000, electrical engineers combined Wi-Fi and Internet to allow us access to it with our portable devices.

Education has benefited tremendously from the Internet. Teachers can supplement their lessons with online material, they can teach remotely, and they can engage with students through chats. Students also have an abundance of information at their fingertips for research.

Even more impressive is the impact on education in countries with few to no resources for educational material. With an Internet connection, teachers can connect with students anywhere in the world and help them get an education they wouldn't otherwise be able to receive.

One interesting organization is the Granny Cloud. Adult volunteers of any age and gender volunteer their time, an hour per week, to provide an online session with a classroom in another part of the world. Grannies are part of a win-win situation: The students get access to education, and the volunteers love being mentors—all thanks to electrical engineers!

MEDICAL TECHNOLOGY

Electrical engineers have played a part in developing medical devices that have saved countless lives, like the implantable cardioverter defibrillator. An ICD is an instrument that is implanted right in the human heart. It sends a small amount of electricity to the heart when needed, preventing a heart attack or heart failure.

Another exciting innovation is the holographic smartphone. A holographic smartphone allows us to see 3D images projected from a smartphone without special glasses. This technology allows users to view images from the sides and behind and interact with them using special hand gestures. The potential implications of such an innovation are powerful in many fields, but especially the medical field. Using 3D holographic images will allow medical professionals to view patients who are not physically with them from different angles. This could lead to lifesaving diagnoses and treatments. Imagine gaining access to medical professionals, experts, and knowledge from around the world to treat medical conditions. Doctors could treat a patient who may be across town, unable to travel due to weather conditions, or too sick to travel or even lives on a different continent. The benefits of this type of smartphone are likely to continue to grow as the technology is perfected and made more affordable and accessible to more individuals and communities.

FIGURE 14: *Diagram of a holographic smartphone for medical use*

FITNESS

Today's smartwatches are great for keeping track of our activity levels. With electronics technology today, some smartwatches can count your steps and convert your activity into number of calories burned. They can also provide a history of how many steps you take per week and alert you to when the number is increasing or decreasing. There are even graphs to use for comparison purposes. From the number of steps, the smartwatch can work out how much oxygen you have in your blood, which can be used to give other information, such as your heart rate. Some smartwatches can also monitor the heart's electrical activity. This is particularly useful if the wearer is prone to heart disease or heart attacks, which it can help detect.

But there is always the potential to do more. In the next decade, many of us may be using even more highly developed smartwatches, such as smartwatches that won't require us to touch the screen or the device itself. Instead, these smartwatches will feature a special ring and sensitive receiver in the form of a bracelet, which can be used to convert touching signals from the skin into the watch. This smartwatch will have the ability to monitor our health, warn us and others if there is danger, and support us in fitness and well-being.

CLEAN ENERGY

As we move from coal- and petroleum-based energy toward clean and renewable energy sources (green energy), such as solar, wind, geothermal, and ocean waves, electrical engineering expertise is becoming very much in demand. Electrical engineers are responsible for designing electrical components, such as software, hardware, wiring, and machinery, for technologies such as wind turbines and solar panels. This includes developing and implementing systems that use electronic equipment to control systems or signal processes.

Geothermal energy is energy from inside Earth. In the crust and the mantle, which is the part of Earth between the crust and the core, are radioactive elements, such as uranium. Radioactive elements give off a lot of heat energy. This heat energy is geothermal energy.

Geothermal energy is an emerging frontier that shows great promise. Sometimes it is obvious where there is a good source, such as near hot springs. Iceland uses geothermal energy to heat almost 100 percent of its homes and businesses.

But this energy is not at consistent depths throughout the world. This makes it challenging to locate and make use of it. Although we might be far off from commercializing this form of energy, green energy is one of the greatest challenges facing us today. The development of geothermal energy could play a large role in meeting global energy needs.

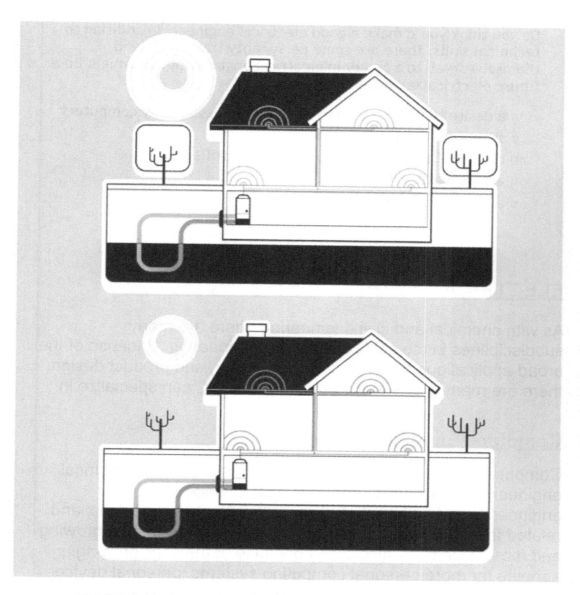

FIGURE 15: *Diagram of geothermal energy to heat a house*

CAREER CHECKLIST

Do you think you'd make a good electrical engineer? In addition to technical skills, there are some personality traits that lend themselves well to a career in electrical engineering. You might be a future electrical engineer if you have:

- a desire to understand how things work, especially computers
- strong communication skills
- creative thinking and problem-solving skills
- a thirst for learning
- a love of science and math

ELECTRICAL ENGINEERING SPECIALTIES

As with chemical and civil engineering, there are many subdisciplines in the field of electrical engineering. Because of the broad applications for electronics, electricity, and product design, there are many areas that electrical engineers can specialize in.

Computer Engineering

Computer engineering is a fascinating combination of electrical engineering, electronics, and computer science. Computer engineers design and develop computing systems, devices, and related technological advances. This is one of the fastest-growing and most in-demand disciplines because of the ever-growing appetite for more personal computing systems, personal devices, and computing tools that allow us to connect faster, more reliably, and for longer periods of time. Computer engineers conduct the research and analysis to determine what is needed in device capabilities with software and hardware to meet the needs of individuals, businesses, and society.

Health care is an area in which computer engineers have made significant contributions. They have developed information systems, data storage systems, and data analyses to help medical professionals. Such information allows for better quality and faster treatment of patients. With the Internet, computer engineers increase worldwide access to medical care, including the ability to engage with world experts.

Communications is such a critical technology today. If you're not familiar with the term "long-distance call," thank a computer engineer. Advances in communications by engineers have made a world that once seemed large and separated into a smaller, more connected place. We now have so many ways to communicate: social media, chatting apps, video calls, virtual business meeting software, and apps that let us communicate with photos. It's almost as if the concept of "long distance" is outdated. Our physical location is no longer a problem in terms of communicating—we can be anywhere and still attend classes or work.

Power Engineering

Power and energy are not the same thing. We use energy to make a change of some kind. Power is how fast we use the energy. For example, an appliance needs a certain amount of power to operate, so much energy per hour. The power of a typical television might be around 230 watts. A power plant converts one type of energy into electrical energy for our use as electricity. Since it can get confusing trying to figure out the difference between energy, power, and electricity, here we just use "power" as an all-encompassing term. Power engineering, or power systems engineering, is often divided into three areas: power generation, power transmission, and power distribution.

Engineers working on power generation are concerned with converting different forms of energy into electrical energy. Whether that energy is obtained from traditional sources, such as fossil fuels or coal, or green methods, such as wind turbines, solar power, ocean waves, or wind power, it must first be converted into electrical energy so we can use it as electricity.

Engineers working on power transmission are concerned with getting the energy from where it is generated to various locations where businesses and consumers can use it.

Power distribution engineers work on the systems that get the energy to consumers and businesses. These systems, which include transformers, generators, motors, and power electronics, have to be developed and maintained in usable voltages for consumers. These engineers are often called "power systems engineers."

Some power engineers work on large systems that are necessary for a city to function and serve its citizens. These engineers generally work on large teams that collaborate to build, maintain, and develop the networks needed to connect the generators and users to a power grid. They work closely with the city's utility companies or local governments to design the components needed for the power grid and maintain the systems.

Some power engineers also work on smaller projects, such as grids that supply smaller plants, perhaps in remote areas, with electricity. It's easy to see how power engineers make the world better by ensuring people can have access to lifesaving and reliable energy sources.

Software Engineering

Software engineering is unique from other branches of engineering. While other engineers generally work on building a physical structure, software engineers develop intangible structures. This does not minimize the importance of software engineering's tangible outcomes. In fact, software can be considered the guidebook, instructions, or operating procedures that are embedded in the machines used in various industries. Properly functioning and innovative software can save lives. Malfunctioning software can have tangible effects—with software used in everything from medical equipment to airplanes, faulty software can result in loss of life.

Software also has to be compatible with all the systems with which it works. One devastating example is a miscommunication that happened with a NASA spacecraft, although fortunately there was no danger to anyone's life or safety. In the late 1990s, NASA launched a spacecraft called the Mars Climate Orbiter. The engineers who designed and built the spacecraft used imperial measurements for acceleration, such as feet per second squared. But the navigation engineers used metric measurements, such as meters per second squared. The result? The spacecraft went sailing past Mars instead of going into orbit around it. Oops.

As a software engineer, you could develop almost any type of software, from a computer game or phone app to more complex software for business systems and applications, operating systems, and network control systems. Software engineers need to learn different programming languages. They also need to be familiar with software development and the computer operating systems on the market.

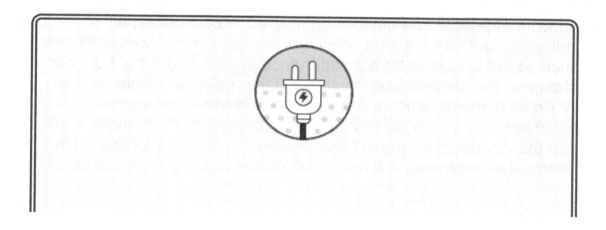

What advice would you give to someone who's thinking about becoming an engineer?

"Never lose your creativity and imagination. You will need to produce great things that are outside the box. Work on problems that you are passionate about or that have major significance in your life. Do not be afraid to ask for help if you need it. Seek out mentors early that are on your career path. If you have the chance to study abroad or go out of the country to connect with other engineers, take the opportunity."

—DR. JESSYE TALLEY, *engineering professor*

Telecommunications Engineering

The Internet of Things (IoT) is the idea of having as many devices as possible connected to the Internet and communicating with each other. The current emphasis on the IoT has elevated today's critical need for telecommunications. The IoT could lead to one enormous network of people and devices connected to each other, all collecting and sharing data. We currently have many conveniences such as being able to let a maintenance person in our front door or changing the temperature inside our home using a remote device. While all of these benefits are genuine, telecommunications engineers must work closely with other professionals to make sure that this connectivity doesn't lead to negative consequences. This means that engineers will need to continue working on solutions to the known risks of hacking, vulnerability, and accessibility to improper devices or for improper use.

Telecommunications has been called the backbone of today's mobile landscape. We send messages to every part of the globe, and the number of ways we do this and the speed at which it happens are always increasing. Telecommunications engineers are responsible for developing and designing communications systems and technologies such as fiber optics, satellite, and traditional wires. They are also responsible for maintaining these systems and keeping them protected from hackers.

Telecommunications engineers can also be involved in product design, development, and installation. This requires the use of scientific theory and telecommunications knowledge to transfer media and design network infrastructure. These engineers also solve problems related to information transfer and Wi-Fi technologies. This means that telecommunications engineers are involved in every part of the process of developing a telecommunications system dealing with both software and hardware.

CHALLENGES IN ELECTRICAL ENGINEERING

An article published by the Institute for Electrical and Electronics Engineers says that the future is "intellectric." What it means is that our usage of electricity should be intelligent in the future. We need to ensure our usage is efficient and safe. Given the breadth of electrical engineering, this is no small challenge. Engineers need to keep up with communications systems. The challenges also include risks to existing electrical power systems, increased consumer demand, new technology trends, and cyberattacks. There are also challenges with artificial intelligence and other innovations that promote and support sustainable development.

The world population is continually growing with a commensurate increase in the demand for electricity. In many parts of the world, this demand is still unmet. The World Energy Council estimates that by 2040 the world's electrical energy needs are expected to be double what they were in 2008. Given the availability of an ever-increasing number of electronic devices, this estimate is likely to increase. As users of these devices, we naturally want to make sure electric energy is reliable and uninterrupted. So not only does the electrical engineering community need to be able to develop new safe, efficient, and reliable ways to deliver this much-needed energy, it also needs to be innovative in the distribution and management of this energy as well as being concerned with the impact any new systems may have on the environment.

LOOKING AHEAD

The discipline of electrical engineering is evolving and continues to expand beyond its foundations. While electronics engineers contribute in many disciplines, the most promising technologies in this field are AI, security, self-driving vehicles, robotics, "big data," and telecommunications.

The expansion of the Internet of Things may be a tremendous discipline boost for the field of electrical engineering. Practicing engineers will need to specialize in areas such as computer programming and telecommunications to ensure the continual application of electrical engineering–related principles to advance society. This means electrical engineering careers will need to adapt to understand software and the circuitry associated with connecting devices to the Internet of Things as well as understand the breadth of the telecommunications industry.

AI is also expected to continue to revolutionize our future. Personal digital assistants are used in billions of households around the world, and that number is only expected to climb. Smart device technologies make it possible for consumers to turn their homes into smart homes that are programmable, remote-controlled, and energy-efficient because of AI learning capabilities. The Nest Learning Thermostat, for instance, learns the user's schedule, habits, and temperature preferences. It then automatically programs itself to meet the consumer's needs. This often leads to more energy-conscious behavior on the part of the consumer. For instance, if the thermostat has "learned" that you are away from home on weekdays between 8:00 a.m. and 6:00 p.m., it may adjust the temperature or turn itself off during that time. Then, a few minutes before you return, it will turn the system back on to your temperature preference. This saves the consumer money on utility bills and reduces energy waste.

The usage of big data is becoming more prevalent. "Big data" refers to the enormous volume of data that we generate by using our smart devices, such as smartphones and smartwatches, all the social media outlets available now, and our online and in-store purchases. We even reveal data when we go through a traffic intersection.

Businesses and organizations love to get their hands on this information. They mine the data for anything that will give them a competitive edge. Health care organizations are able to help patients sooner with access to the right information. Another application is the ability to recommend a product to a consumer based on that person's history of usage.

Perhaps the most common application so far of big data usage is targeted advertising. Social media sites, e-commerce platforms, and streaming services use the data we generate every time we use the service. They use this information to make recommendations as to what we might like to watch, based on our viewing history, but they also use our information to provide ads for products that they think will appeal to us.

Work in Progress

Electrical engineering has made considerable contributions in the medical device community. If you think of the brain as a complex electrical circuit, as an electrical engineer you can study how to manipulate that circuit to repair damaged electrical connections and improve function.

One innovative area of focus is in ophthalmological prosthetics (artificial devices related to the eye). According to the World Health Organization, in 2010 there were about 39 million people with some form of visual impairment. This encompasses different diseases and conditions, such as age-related macular degeneration and retinitis pigmentosa.

In order for us to see anything, light reflected from an object first enters our eyes. The photoreceptor cells in the retina detect the light, and the retina processes the information and sends it to the brain. As a result, we see the object. However, the photoreceptors in some people with a visual impairment either are damaged or don't work, and those people cannot see well.

For more than a decade, researchers at Stanford University have been developing an artificial retina (a computer chip) that can be implanted in the eye to allow visually impaired individuals to see again. A surgeon attaches a tiny array, or chip, to the retina. A miniature camera attached to a pair of glasses takes an image of an object and sends the image to the array. The array uses the camera's signals to get the retina cells activated and the image sent to the brain. In order for the person to be able to see the object, there have to be some retina cells that are still working.

There are many challenges associated with developing such an innovative device. For example, the tiny computer chip generates heat energy when it processes information. Visual data must be processed and transmitted from the camera to the artificial retina and on to the brain in order to make an image and allow the person to see. There is so much data that is necessary in this process that engineers and scientists believe that the computer chip may heat up too much and damage the eye.

However, researchers have recently identified a way to process this information by using less data. By using less data, there is less work in the implanted chip, so the chip stays cooler and won't damage the eye. This innovation is still in development, but it is very promising. Tests have shown that the underlying idea works. One patient had a test implant and could see light but not distinct shapes —so more research and tests are needed. New materials and technology improvements will continue to help electrical engineers and eye specialists fine-tune this device.

FIGURE 16: *Diagram of an artificial retina*

Chapter 5
MECHANICAL ENGINEERING

INSPIRING INNOVATION

If you are looking for a personal mode of transportation for short trips or to zip around town, researchers at the University of Tokyo may have a solution on the horizon for you. These engineering and science researchers have designed a portable and inflatable e-bike that fits in a backpack so it can be taken on public transportation. This e-bike was developed to be an efficient way to travel short and medium distances with a maximum speed of about 4 to 5 miles per hour.

The bike, called Poimo (for POrtable and Inflatable MObility), can be inflated with a small pump into a comfortable, safe mobility system or motorbike. Poimo is being developed by student engineers at the University of Tokyo. The bike is constructed from thermoplastic polyurethane and can be inflated in about 60 seconds with the pump. After inflating the bike, the rider attaches the wheels, motor, battery, and wireless controller. The total mass of these items is about 2.5 pounds. The total mass of the bike itself is only around 12 pounds, making the bike lightweight and safer for riders and pedestrians than traditional motorized bikes. Since it can be deflated and folded into a backpack, there is no need to carry a heavy bike lock or worry about storing the bike outside where it is vulnerable to theft and the elements.

The motor is electric, so the bike has advantages similar to electric cars in terms of polluting the environment—no toxic emissions. If thousands of people in busy cities such as Tokyo traded their cars for Poimos, there could be significantly less pollution from vehicles going into the atmosphere. This also improves air quality and helps preserve the ozone layer. This type of creative and out-of-the-box thinking is what the world needs to help solve some of the environmental crises facing us today.

There are advantages to parking, too. You don't have to park a Poimo at all; you just take it with you in a backpack. Further, since it's so light, the small battery doesn't have to work hard, so it should have a decent interval between charges.

There is interest in the type of plastic used to make Poimos. It is sturdy and could perhaps be used in other applications, such as a portable chair or couch. Bringing your own seating to a sports event or other outdoor event in this way could be very popular!

The real motivation for developing Poimo was the desire to use soft robotics techniques to produce a safe vehicle that reduces the potential for injury or damage in case there's an accident. Soft robotics is making robotic devices from bendable materials, similar to living tissue. This is important for personal mobility systems that operate in spaces shared by pedestrians, such as crowded city streets and college campuses.

As a mechanical engineer, it may be your job to experiment with this type of technology and think through other possible soft robotics applications. Could you use this technology to design an inflatable car? Or perhaps a mobile home? Think of the applications for makeshift shelters, disaster relief tents, and temporary refugee communities. All the world's problems can be solved with the right engineering mindset.

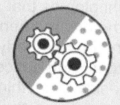

What advice would you give to someone who's thinking about becoming an engineer?

> *"Don't be discouraged if you fail your first exam or don't understand something. All of my professors encouraged asking questions in office hours and expect people to improve over time. I have done terribly on exam 1 and then got an A on the final. Just push yourself through and extinguish any doubt. Ask friends for help, form study groups, and make sure you take breaks. I always walk away from a project or homework when I get stuck or don't understand. I take a break, do something enjoyable, and then come back and I always have a different approach and solution."*
>
> **—JULIA ESPOSITO,** *project engineer*

DEEP DIVE

Mechanical engineers study systems and objects in motion. Therefore, they work on technologies that affect everyone's lives—equipment, transportation, the environment, space exploration, climate change, and even the human body. From toys and roller coasters to bikes and cars to air and spacecraft, mechanical engineers have a hand in basically anything we use in our lives that moves. Creators and problem solvers, those who choose to study mechanical engineering are truly on a track to change the world.

By combining creativity, math, science, analytical tools, and physical technologies, mechanical engineers can shape an idea into reality. The subject areas that form the main basis for a mechanical engineer's knowledge are math, science, mechanics (the physics of motion), energy transfer and conversion, design, and manufacturing. Through the innovative use of analysis, modeling, and design, mechanical engineers solve important problems to improve quality of life, promote sustainability, and even improve health care for people around the world. For example, a mechanical engineer might work on creating a prosthetic limb, collaborate with an electrical engineer to build a surgical robot, or even use their knowledge of fluid dynamics to study how blood flows through damaged or narrowed blood vessels.

Some of the main industries in which you'll find mechanical engineers are the automotive, computing, electronics, robotics, automation, biotechnology, aerospace, mechanical, and manufacturing industries. There are many more; the American Society of Mechanical Engineers lists more than 30 related areas, demonstrating the breadth and diversity of the field.

As a mechanical engineer, you'll have an opportunity to apply your science, math, and technology knowledge, as well as your creative problem-solving skills, to join teams that develop and produce systems and devices. The development process includes analyzing and troubleshooting any systems you work on, either new systems and devices or those already in place that need updating or improving. Perhaps you will be part of a team involved in developing new spacecraft, creating a new renewable energy technology, or improving a transportation technology. There's a world of possibilities out there for aspiring mechanical engineers!

What They Can Do

It would be difficult to identify an aspect of our daily lives that is not touched by mechanical engineering. Mechanical engineers design and make all kinds of devices and technologies, such as microsensors, medical devices, computers, electric cars, robots, sports equipment, drones, and airplanes.

A mechanical engineer might work in areas associated with health, safety, sustainability, and product design. The work of mechanical engineers also significantly impacts the environment, for example, with pollution detection equipment devices, cleanup strategies, and improving manufacturing processes to reduce the amount of waste or runoff into nearby rivers and streams. Here are some industries in which mechanical engineers can be especially useful.

ROBOTICS

Robots help us by completing tasks that we either cannot or would rather not complete, so they can make some jobs safer and other jobs less tedious. Mechanical engineers who work in robotics are responsible for developing robotic systems and devices to help us. In the manufacturing industry in particular, robots can make systems more efficient. In addition to understanding the mechanics of robotics, robotics engineers design the systems so that they are productive and safe to operate. Important skills to have in this field are being able to use computer-aided design, computer-aided manufacturing systems, and drafting skills. There is a research component here, too; some engineers research other systems and methods to ensure their new systems are cost-effective and efficient.

Robotic technology is very important in the space program, and not just in probes and rovers that go to other planets. On the International Space Station, different robots help the astronauts lift and move materials.

SUSTAINABILITY AND ENERGY STORAGE

One of the sustainable development goals of the United Nations is ensuring access to affordable, reliable, and sustainable energy. Mechanical engineers are well suited to be at the forefront of advancing this goal. For example, researchers and students at the University of Washington Mechanical Engineering Department are currently working together with local industry to develop next-generation renewable energy technologies, such as marine, solar, and wind. They are also studying ways to integrate these clean energy sources into the electrical grid and store electrical energy as well. Their work aims to improve the environment. The new partnerships are proving to be effective in reducing pollution and promoting clean combustion.

While developing alternative sources of energy is necessary, it is also necessary to improve energy-storage devices. Battery technology continues to improve, but better batteries are still needed to store energy produced by alternative energy sources. Mechanical engineers in Scotland at a private company called Gravitricity are really putting their creativity to work. They are developing an energy-storage system using input electricity, gravity, heavy weights, and an abandoned mine shaft.

The engineers attach huge masses, up to 11 million pounds each, to cables, which are operated with a winch. The weights are raised and lowered in an abandoned mine shaft, so the depth can be up to 5,000 feet. When raising the weights, the system generates energy and charges itself. When lowering the weights, the energy is discharged to provide electricity to local homes and businesses.

ASSISTIVE TECHNOLOGY DESIGN

Technology has been significant in improving independence, access, and quality of life for individuals with disabilities. Much of this is accomplished through innovations called assistive technology devices. Assistive technology is any technology—equipment, a prosthetic, some software—that improves the lives of people who live with a disability. Current estimates are that more than a million people around the world need an assistive device to communicate or get around. However, according to the World Health Organization, 90 percent of those people do not have access to these often life-changing devices. Studying mechanical engineering will be a foundation to support the research, design, and development of assistive technologies.

Every year, the Massachusetts Institute of Technology hosts the Assistive Technology Hackathon. The purpose is to promote innovation in this area so students will come up with useful technologies. During the Hackathon, students develop their technology solutions to problems faced by citizens with disabilities in the Boston area. Students are given 24 hours to prototype assistive devices to meet the needs of a person with a disability.

Students have shared that, in addition to technical and engineering knowledge, it is equally important to communicate with the user of the device. You need to ensure that you truly understand the user's needs driving this innovation. Therefore, it is important to have strong communication skills as well as academic and technological skills. This is a growing field with many opportunities for engineers to work across multiple industries and countries to meet the needs of individuals with disabilities worldwide.

HEALTH CARE

Some universities are offering mechanical engineering programs with the ability to specialize in health care. In this field, mechanical engineers can work at designing hospitals and clinics, sophisticated diagnostic equipment, or innovative medical devices. In all cases, having strong problem-solving skills is important.

There are special challenges to be met while designing a hospital. The engineers must be on top of all the guidelines and hospital-specific building codes. The ventilation system has to be top-notch, too, to prevent contaminants and toxins from reaching the staff and patients.

A mechanical engineering team at Stanford University has developed a medical device to help diagnose eye problems. It uses a smartphone's built-in camera to take images of the retina and optic nerve. To accomplish this, researchers developed an adapter that holds a smartphone and also has a magnification lens. The lens peers into the eye, while the adapter holds a smartphone camera at just the right distance from the lens in order to take a picture of the magnified image of the inner eye.

This innovative use of mechanical engineering knowledge to address a medical need allows medical practitioners to take eye scans and transmit them online to a specialist for diagnosis. One of the developers, Assistant Professor Dr. Robert Chang, suggests thinking of this as Instagram for the eye.

SPORTS

If you're a mechanical engineer with a love of sports, you can certainly combine your work and play. Designing and developing sports equipment is one area in which mechanical engineers are needed. To do this, understanding anatomy and how the body works is a great background. Engineers who work on developing new sports equipment have to test everything before putting anything on the market. With all the new materials being introduced, an engineer may have a lot to choose from to try different things.

There is much research involved in designing sports equipment. Engineers must be able to see how a player's or athlete's body moves and reacts with the equipment and the playing environment. This can all be viewed on recorded sports games, where the engineer can stop, rewind, play slow motion, and so on, to be able to analyze all motions and reactions. Such information can help reduce potential injuries with new equipment. Of course, all new products and prototypes can be modeled with computer simulations.

Another area is designing new sports facilities. This could involve understanding how different surfaces for playing fields or courts affect the ability of the players to run, jump, and bounce basketballs.

Mechanical engineers can be involved in the development and manufacture of new sports clothing, too. The engineer may help test different fabrics or design the machines and systems to manufacture the items.

ELECTRONICS

Mechanical engineers are typically involved in designing machines, for example, vehicles, home appliances, elevators, generators, and tools. With electronics playing such a large part in so many technologies, newer, better, and smaller sensors are becoming more and more desirable. Sensors are devices that detect signals and convert them to electrical energy. The signal could be a temperature reading, a measurement of the magnetic field, a sound, or even a humidity reading. Microsensors are tiny sensors, up to about a fifth of an inch wide.

Mechanical engineers are always trying to improve microsensors and incorporate them into whatever machine systems or technology they are designing. These microsensors are prevalent in many of our personal electronic devices. Shahrzad Towfighian is an associate professor of mechanical engineering at Binghamton University in New York. She and her team have developed a new way to make microsensors. Researchers suggest that her method may revolutionize the microsensor industry because the new microsensors will be more reliable, especially in microphones in cell phones, for example. She plans to combine this advance with existing actuator technologies, which will reduce the background noise produced by some electronics. (An actuator is a component of a mechanical system that helps something move.) She is also looking ahead to how the new method can be applied in other technologies, such as pressure sensors.

CAREER CHECKLIST

Some of the most important skills and preparations for success as a mechanical engineer aren't things you would go to school for. You could be a great mechanical engineer someday if you:

o love math and science

o are interested in what makes something work

o have the ability to work under pressure

o use creative problem-solving skills

o are happy working with others

o have strong verbal and written communication skills

MECHANICAL ENGINEERING SPECIALTIES

Because of the breadth of this field of study, society relies quite a bit on mechanical engineers. With such a high demand, there are many opportunities for new mechanical engineers. Here are just some of the many areas you can specialize in.

Automotive Engineering

Automotive engineering is one of the most exciting, challenging, and rewarding career fields. Automotive engineers are concerned with the development and design of passenger cars, trucks, buses, motorcycles, and off-road vehicles. They also work on the self-driving vehicles being developed today. Every time someone touches a car, they are being impacted by the work of an automotive engineer. These engineers may design new products or modify existing ones, troubleshoot, and solve engineering problems associated with an automotive system and plan. They also evaluate and design vehicles for safety. Some also design manufacturing processes to efficiently produce the finished product.

Industrial Engineering

Industrial and systems engineers design and oversee installation of various integrated systems of equipment, people, and information. This field of study draws on specialized skills in math, social sciences, physical sciences, and medicine as well as engineering principles to develop systems.

Industrial engineers who focus on people at work or in product design are called ergonomists, or human factors engineers. Broadly, ergonomics is the study of people physically interacting in their workplace. Industrial engineers who focus on ergonomics apply traditional engineering knowledge and principles, as well as knowledge of the human body, to design safe, efficient systems, processes, and equipment. Areas that these engineers may work in include designing automobile seating, aircraft interior design, cell phone layout and design, and processes and equipment used by health care professionals.

Why did you want to become an engineer?

"It all started with my dad taking me with him to the production warehouse where he was working as an

electrical engineer. There, I had a chance to learn about systems and products. But I didn't even like math until high school, where one of my teachers was different than others in the way she explained it. Everything after that started being clearer. I learned that I could concentrate more on the areas I enjoyed, rather than following curriculums blindly, so I choose electives accordingly and didn't mind changing tracks from the physics department to systems engineering. I knew that I liked studying systems, but that was very broad, so I tried to enroll in internship/co-ops in different engineering fields to learn what I liked and what I didn't. I always had mentors and role models who guided me through all these trials and errors. Looking back now, it was all worth it! I can say I love the work I do and am proud of the type of engineer I became."

—DR. ASLI AKBAS, *systems engineer*

Acoustical Engineering

Acoustical engineers are dedicated to the study of sound and vibration, typically the design, analysis, and control of sound. This might mean applying acoustics, the science of sound and vibration, to improve sound quality by limiting unwanted background noise. Conversely, an acoustical engineer may want to highlight the quality of a certain sound. Acoustical engineers also work with sound at frequencies that we cannot hear. For example, ultrasound waves can be used as a technique to locate fatigue cracks, allowing engineers to diagnose and prevent mechanical failures without damaging the part in question.

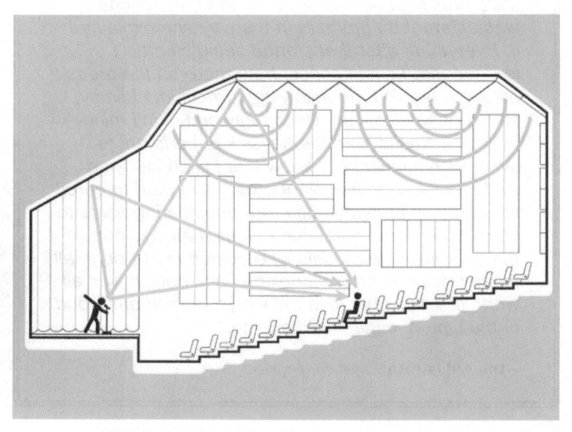

FIGURE 17: *Diagram of sound reflection in a theater*

If you choose to become an acoustical engineer, you could be working with others to design stadiums, concert halls, recording studios, or even meeting rooms. The Acoustical Society of America lists various subdisciplines in this area: architectural acoustics, physical acoustics, noise control, underwater acoustics, and more. With underwater acoustics, sound waves can be emitted from a ship and aimed toward the bottom of an ocean or lake. Different materials have different properties, such as how they reflect or absorb light and sound. Engineers can use the returned sound signal to help identify the geological materials and identify buried cables.

Given the importance of sound to musicians, it's not surprising that many students who pursue graduate programs in acoustics also come from some sort of musical background. If you have a passion for music or singing, you could easily incorporate it into your career as an acoustical engineer!

Aerospace Engineering

Aerospace engineers design any machine that flies. They also develop, test, and produce the machines as well as any related systems. The machine could be a missile, a spacecraft, a spacecraft's rocket—any equipment related to the machine's flight.

Aerospace engineering is a newer branch of engineering. Although humans have been interested in flight at least since da Vinci's drawings of a flying machine in 1485, the field of aerospace engineering didn't emerge until the 1800s. That's when the first experiments in flight took place. It didn't take long for two specialties to appear. Aeronautical engineers work with flight technologies that do not go into space: airplanes, helicopters, and high-speed aircraft. Astronautical engineers work with flight technologies that focus on spacecraft. Worldwide interest in flight has propelled expansion of this field, often with the financial support and interest of government and federal agencies.

FIGURE 18: *Diagram of a helicopter design*

The Mars rovers are examples of sophisticated aerospace innovations. The rovers were designed and built on Earth to survive in a completely different environment—Mars. Imagine the conditions engineers have to understand to make something like this work: very little atmosphere, no oxygen (so no combustion engines), a reduced gravity environment (about 40 percent of Earth's gravity), dust storms, reliance on solar energy for power but less solar energy than on Earth, and more. And once the rovers landed safely on Mars, they had to collect information and send it back to Earth. These rovers are quite an engineering feat!

Manufacturing Engineering

Almost everything we use in our daily lives is fabricated or manufactured, from our shoes to our cars. For these products to be manufactured, a manufacturing engineer has to be involved. Manufacturing engineers focus on designing and operating integrated systems that produce high-quality, economically competitive, and safe products. These systems combine multiple processes, including computer networks, robots, tools, and material handling equipment. First, a manufacturing engineer designs a product. Next, they decide on the best processes to make the product. A manufacturing engineer can also be involved in planning and designing the factories that will produce the product. Finally, manufacturing engineers oversee the daily operations, quality control, management, maintenance, and improvement of the manufacturing facility.

Since we live in an age of such rapid innovation and complex technology, opportunities for manufacturing engineers are growing. Each innovation for a new product or form of technology will require manufacturing for some, if not all, aspects of the product.

CHALLENGES IN MECHANICAL ENGINEERING

Some of the biggest challenges in mechanical engineering may be in the oil and gas industry. In most cases, projects in the oil and gas industry involve the design and construction of new pipelines. If done improperly, the project can cost billions of dollars in economic loss. In addition to the financial risks associated with large projects, there are great risks to the environment. Understanding how to properly design pipelines and other aspects of oil and gas delivery is a critical area for mechanical engineers. Accidents involving oil and gas leaks are hugely detrimental to residents and the environment.

As we've discussed in previous chapters, access to clean water remains one of the most pressing needs throughout the world. In addition to the issues related to water mentioned earlier in this book, engineers also work to ensure that contaminants don't get into our drinking water. In 2014, citizens in Flint, Michigan, learned that lead had seeped into their drinking water after the city changed the source of its water supply. Lead in drinking water is incredibly harmful. High levels of lead, especially for children and pregnant women, can lead to health problems and learning disabilities. When people learned about the lead in Flint, there was a huge public health crisis. People couldn't use the water! This dire situation led to an extensive service line replacement effort. Mechanical engineers are integral to these efforts, working with the government and public health officials to ensure that the water supply is again clean and safe for its citizens.

Another challenge is developing alternative sources of energy as well as new capabilities for energy storage. Mechanical engineers will be looking into new ways to store energy as well as new materials to use in batteries. Lithium-ion batteries are good, but they don't last long enough. They also generate a lot of heat energy. This type of battery is good for powering smaller devices, but something better is needed to store energy for larger uses, especially from alternative energy sources, such as solar and wind energy. If consumers use solar or wind energy to power their homes, what happens when it's cloudy? When it's nighttime? When there's no wind? They have to rely on previously stored energy.

With a typical system using solar panels, excess energy goes back to the grid, so when a homeowner needs a supplement, say, during the night, they can access it. More and more consumers want to store their excess energy themselves, though. There are systems for this, but they are still in development.

Keep in mind, it took about 40 years for the development of the lithium-ion battery, so it is never too soon to start developing new or improving current technology!

LOOKING AHEAD

To be prepared to solve the world's problems, future mechanical engineers will need to be skilled in product design, they will need to understand the most pressing needs in society, and they will need to be aware of the environmental impact of their engineering designs. As new materials are introduced and new technologies developed, mechanical engineers will be faced with new opportunities and require new skills.

Mechanical engineers will be developing systems, processes, and innovations that can efficiently and effectively clean water and deliver it around the world. Researchers around the country and the world are working on systems that use solar power and other environmentally friendly approaches to clean and desalinate water.

The importance of advancing alternative energy sources and improving energy-storage capabilities cannot be overstated. The planet is out of balance—there is too much pollution going into the atmosphere from technologies using fossil fuels. The pollution contributed by vehicles and industry was made very clear when the COVID-19 pandemic first hit the United States in full force during the spring of 2020. Satellite images clearly showed a huge decline in pollutants as the pandemic took hold, when there were far fewer drivers on the roads and less industrial pollution.

Mechanical engineers choosing to work in this field will be collaborating with numerous other professionals: environmental engineers, economists, chemical engineers, electrical engineers, software engineers, and more. They will help design and build new laboratories for testing, develop new procedures and tests, develop new software and simulations, improve fuel cell technology, develop new technologies, improve machine efficiency, and invent new sensors and microsensors.

Related to the energy field is the study of climate change. Mechanical engineers will be involved by helping to develop tests and sensors to monitor the conditions of local climates and the atmosphere.

Another area of focus will be biomechanics. Engineers in this field will be designing new medical devices and equipment, exploring biological processes, and discovering new ways to help hospitals and clinics treat their patients. They will be depending on modeling and simulation software. Mechanical engineers can supplement their education and training with strong biology and computer science studies.

As all areas of mechanical engineering develop, the uniting thread will continue to be the computer. Engineers have to be comfortable with more than just the basics, such as email, Internet searching, and office management software. Engineers will be using simulations more and more to test concepts and simulate some situations and experiments instead of performing them in a lab. They can simulate physical processes, such as air flow, and they can simulate designs using nanomaterials. Some of this demand is driven by competition. Using simulations can reduce the amount of time needed for actual tests and allow a technology to become available sooner.

Work in Progress

Agriculture is one of the building blocks of our civilization. Over thousands of years, we have been using technology to grow food effectively and safely and to care for livestock. One ongoing area of research and development in this field is the use of drones.

While drones have a multitude of uses, the agricultural industry uses them as a part of an effective approach to sustainable agricultural management. Drones can provide data and real-time images and can have extensive monitoring technologies—so agricultural engineers and farmers can use drones to help streamline their operations and gain insights into their crops.

The use of drones has the potential to enhance agricultural engineering and transform the way crops are grown, managed, and distributed. While drones have not made it into mainstream agriculture yet, they play an increasingly important role in precision farming, helping agricultural professionals lead the way with sustainable farming practices while also protecting and increasing output and profitability.

Crops face dramatic losses due to insects, fungi, weeds, and other pests. Drones have the potential to be effective in targeting and treating pest outbreaks or hotspots in crops. This is particularly important in countries like India, where more than 70 percent of the rural population depends on agriculture for food and work. Agricultural blights reduce the productivity of the crops and affect the well-being of these communities. Pesticides and fertilizers are used to kill the insects and to enhance the crop quality. However, the World Health Organization estimates that a million individuals get sick every year from spraying pesticides manually. So, having drones instead of people spraying pesticides also protects laborers.

Precision agricultural technologies such as drones can offer important opportunities for integrated pest management. Experts in agricultural engineering agree that sustainable agricultural practices should increasingly depend on drones and other innovative technologies to support remote sensing, visual inspection, and insect outbreak prevention.

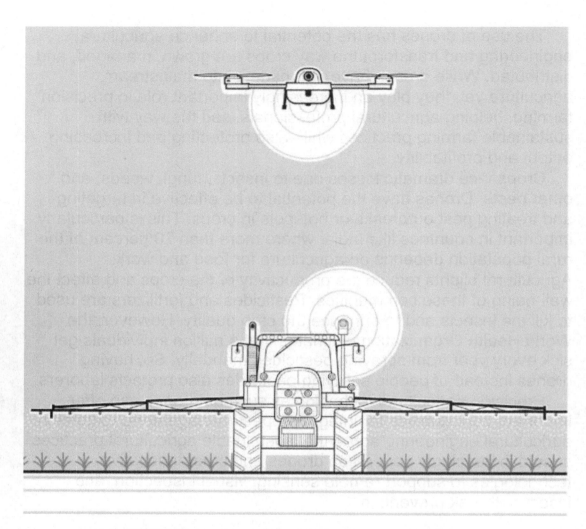

FIGURE 19: *Diagram of drone use in agriculture*

Chapter 6
PUTTING IT TOGETHER

NOW THAT YOU HAVE LEARNED about the different areas of engineering, you have a good idea of what engineering looks like and what engineers do. I hope you are excited about the impact that you can have on the world as an engineer.

One thing for sure is that you will never be bored in an engineering career. Engineering is a constantly evolving and changing profession, and we need bright and creative minds such as yours to help us move the world forward to a brighter future for us all. Also, as you think about your engineering career, please think beyond the borders of your country. Engineers work across borders to make a difference for people and communities all over the world. Engineers are needed to solve the world's problems and to develop new products, services, and resources that help address many challenges, including engineering's grand challenges and the United Nations Sustainable Development Goals mentioned earlier.

Quiz: What Kind of Engineer Should I Be?

At this point, you may be wondering what kind of engineer you should become. That is a common situation students find themselves in when learning of the many opportunities in engineering. The following quiz will help you determine which engineering discipline might be the best fit for you.

For each question, select the answer that best describes your thoughts and ideas as they relate to your engineering career.

1. **Which activity would you rather spend the evening working on as a project?**

   A. Designing a water filter for home use that includes filtration materials to remove pollutants from tap water

   B. Building a bridge made out of spaghetti that can hold up to five pounds

   C. Designing a system that turns on the lights when a person enters the room and turns them off when the person leaves

   D. Designing an automatic dog-feeding machine that serves the food and cleans the dog's bowl afterward

2. **Select the class project that you think you would enjoy the most.**

   A. Exploring food production problems related to population growth around the world

   B. Designing, building, and testing a small dome that supports a quarter of a pound

   C. Building a circuit that detects ripe produce in the grocery store

D. Measuring the amount of force on an amusement park ride

3. **Which field trip best describes one you would like to take?**

   A. An engineering field trip to a perfume design laboratory or pharmaceutical lab

   B. A trip to view bridges that won the design-of-the-year contest

   C. A trip to the local power plant to see how electricity is distributed to your neighborhood

   D. A trip to a drone design and manufacturing facility

4. **Which activity would you do if you had the time and money available?**

   A. Design a chemical process that turns a strip of paper pink in the presence of the flu

   B. Design an aquarium that is a temporary home for an injured manatee

   C. Design a computer program that helps you select the college you want to attend based on your criteria

D. Design a solar energy system to heat your swimming pool

5. **Which of these sounds like the most fun to you?**

   A. Inventing a solution that keeps your cell phone screen and case from absorbing water

   B. Designing a pathway from your home to your school especially for motorized scooter riders

   C. Developing a computer app that helps you recall where information is stored during an exam

D. Building a robot to do all of your household chores

6. **Which classes or topics do you or would you enjoy the most?**

    A. Chemistry or biology

    B. Drafting, design, or architecture

    C. Computer programming

    D. Mechanical design

7. **Which of the following jobs can you most easily see yourself doing?**

    A. Working in a company to design substances that help fresh produce last longer

    B. Designing the layout of a city and all of its highways

    C. Designing computer software apps

    D. Working on airplane or rocket design

8. **Which of the following projects excites you the most?**

    A. Doing a project on the role of engineers in creating lawn pesticides that do not harm pets

    B. Designing a model for a sturdy home in areas where hurricanes strike

    C. Building a circuit to measure the strength of a magnetic field produced by two magnets

    D. Designing motor scooters for safe use by children

9. **If you had to watch a video to learn a new skill, which of these skills would you learn?**

   A. Determining how different vitamins affect people's energy and mood levels

   B. Determining the best materials to design a racetrack for go-carts

   C. Learning how to use outside smoke detectors with electrical sensors to detect the early start of forest fires

   D. Learning how roller coasters are designed

10. **Which of the following health care projects would you want to be involved in?**

   A. Developing a test to determine whether a person is allergic to a specific dog breed

   B. Designing and converting a bus into a mobile hospital for homeless individuals

   C. Building a heart rate monitor that can be read remotely

   D. Designing an electronic brace to help people with disabilities walk

NOW, TALLY YOUR RESULTS:

A	B	C	D

Mostly "a." Responses: You are probably well aligned with the discipline of chemical engineering. Keep in mind that chemical engineering has related fields, such as biomedical, biochemical, environmental, and materials engineering. This field also includes the growing area of nuclear engineering.

Mostly "b." Responses: Consider a career in civil engineering. Civil engineering is a broad discipline that includes construction, environmental, geotechnical, urban, and transportation engineering. You'll have many exciting options here to put your knowledge, skills, and passion to good use.

Mostly "c." Responses: You would make a great electrical engineer. Electrical engineers can also work in power, software, computer, and telecommunications engineering. You'll find a lot of opportunity in this space, especially as the world becomes more and more connected through the Internet.

Mostly "d." Responses: Mechanical engineering could be the right branch for you. Mechanical engineering has multiple related disciplines, such as aerospace, manufacturing, and industrial engineering. Within these areas, you'll have an opportunity to impact the world and often work more closely with people than in some other engineering disciplines.

Don't be surprised if you found an even split in your responses. You could be a great fit for either of those majors. You may also want to consider selecting one engineering discipline for your major and studying the other as a minor in college. Engineers work closely across disciplines. Often you will find yourself doing things that are related to other engineering disciplines. If you find yourself in this position, you'll have an opportunity to use various interests across the different fields of engineering.

CONGRATULATIONS!

I hope you can now see the exciting, satisfying, and fun opportunities to make a difference in the world as an engineer. Congratulations and welcome to your future! This will be a fun and exciting yet challenging and sometimes demanding academic path. But you can do this. You have what it takes to be an engineer. Be sure to use the resources and support systems available to you as you prepare to become an engineer. Remember the stories we've shared of young people who were just like you a few years ago? They became engineers. You can, too.

Engineering is a challenging college major, and there will probably be tough times as you study for exams. There might be some courses that you wish you didn't have to take. This is true of pretty much any college major. When those difficult courses come along or you face challenges—and maybe even failure—please hold on to your dream. This may mean getting support from tutors, mentors, or your professors. It's a great idea to do this even when your classes are going well. Engineering is a challenging major, but it is definitely worth the effort.

Finally, I want to encourage you to stay focused and eager to achieve your goal of becoming an engineer, no matter what challenges come your way. Don't let academic challenges, financial challenges, or anything else get in your way. We are here to support you in your journey. Make sure you connect with professional societies, mentors, tutors, and your professors along the way.

Above all, don't quit! Don't give up on your engineering dreams.

Made in the USA
Middletown, DE
05 June 2024

55289260R00077